Olivette R. Swallen

Fall 1962

About the Author

Thirty years of living and working in the Orient have given Andrew T. Roy a wealth of knowledge and experience on which to draw in writing of the people on Asia's rim. He has traveled extensively in each of the areas of which he writes.

On the mainland of China he served as teacher and student worker in universities at Chung-tu and Nanking. For two years he lived under the present Communist government of China. At present, as a fraternal worker for the United Presbyterian Church in the U.S.A., he is vice president of Chung Chi College in Hong Kong. This is an interdenominational college of arts and sciences founded in 1950 to continue the traditions of the former thirteen Chinese Christian mainland universities. Fifty per cent of the students are refugees from China; many are Hong Kong residents; and each year brings some from Chinese communities in Indonesia, Borneo, Sarawak, and Malaya.

A graduate of Washington and Lee University, Dr. Roy earned his Ph.D. at Princeton. He has studied also in Edinburgh and Oxford. He is the author of **Risk and Hope: the Hong Kong Story.**

FRIENDSHIP PRESS   NEW YORK

ON
ASIA'S
RIM

*** BY ***
ANDREW T. ROY

Friendship Press · New York

Library of Congress Catalog Card Number: 62–7848

CONTENTS

FOREWORD

This book will have a different effect upon different readers. It is not solely a success story. Rather it is an honest attempt to report on conditions that can be checked by any of you. Some of the facts will be out of date by the time the book goes to press, but this is to be expected when dealing with an area of such rapid social change. Some readers may be depressed by the picture, for conditions on the rim of East Asia are indeed alarming. Others may feel encouraged, for the situation contains elements of great hope. It is no service to the church or the public to hide dangerous facts behind the innocent, the good, and the optimistic.

We believe in Jesus Christ and in the work that he is continuing through his church. It would be a disservice to him who was the Truth to falsify or overglorify the human effort that offers an imperfect witness to what life in obedience to him is like and what believing in him involves.

The problems confronting the church in its mission are tremendous; its agents are human, and its opponents are imposing. The prayer and thought and participation of all who take Christ's name are needed if we are to move through the present array of problems to fairer weather and a straight course ahead.

ANDREW T. ROY

THE RIM
OF EAST ASIA

THE ISLANDS BETWEEN

Between the great circles of American influence, stretching from Alaska to the Philippines, and of Soviet-Chinese influence, extending from Siberia to North Vietnam, are 38 million people crowded onto peninsulas and islands of sharply limited size and resources. These areas are under ideological tension and pressure from both sides and have their full quota of human suffering and heroic action. Most of their inhabitants, however, are not enthusiastically committed to martyrdom, but, like North Americans, they would settle for a free life and a reasonable measure of security. Among these are 15 million refugees who hope that their present status and apparent destiny are not final.

Through the accident of their geographic location, Korea, Okinawa, Taiwan (also known as Formosa), and Hong Kong are forced into a strategic importance they did not choose. Their problems, in origin and extent, are not localized but are world wide. They have a claim upon the attention and concern of all men who retain a conscience or who have some imagination with regard to the future.

This is not the first time in history that small areas have

assumed a crucial importance, holding the key to war or peace for larger neighbors. Greece, Luxembourg, Poland, Tunisia, or postwar Berlin are examples. Such areas, being the crossroads of moving cultures, are subject to the contrary magnetic pull of different power fields and are watched with intense interest by the whole world. They serve as barometers of the international weather, providing storm warnings and registering periods of high and low pressure. Occasionally, they prove to be laboratories in which solutions are found for problems of cultural and political conflict. More often, they are used as show windows for competing ways of life. If order is preserved and tempers kept cool, incidents of reconciliation can occur as well as incidents that touch off conflict. It is from such areas that we should expect new insights, new experimental approaches. The alternatives are many, the resources varied, the choices open. Thank God for small buffer areas between great aggressive systems!

The misfortune of those born in these "islands between" is that they are cast by the interests of others for roles that they did not seek, and they are forced to appear on the world's stage when most of them would prefer privacy and humble seats in the second balcony. Like the woman who touched the hem of Christ's garment, they want the healing flow of world concern and aid without the loss of anonymity or the necessity of public decision. In our concern for them, it is not enough to think of them as important simply because they are important to *us* at the moment, expendable in the defense of "our way of life." Korea, Okinawa, Taiwan, and Hong Kong are important in God's eyes, regardless of their relation to our destiny and immediate struggle. If the Shepherd left ninety-nine sheep to hunt for one, perhaps God doesn't think that 180 million people in the U.S.A. are a dearer concern to him than the 38 million on the rim of East Asia who have been left in an exposed position by recent international storms.

Therefore, though these particular Asian peoples are in a strategic situation and capable of making contributions to others beyond normal expectation, such considerations are only secondary ones for the Christian church. Were there no cold war, no divided world, and no struggle for the mind of Asia, the church, if obedient and sensitive, would still care as much and do as much as it would with its eye on the newspapers and its ear to the radio.

The present relevance of concern for the people on the rim of East Asia cannot be disregarded, however, since their location adds greatly to the complexity of their own problems. Though with true disinterestedness you bear the Korean, Okinawan, Taiwan, and Hong Kong peoples before God in your love and prayer and thought, you will still find that, because of recent history and special pressures, these countries are intimately related to decisions made in Peking, Moscow, Tokyo, Washington, Ottawa, London, and the United Nations. The church cannot be abstracted entirely from the context of such decisions.

All men are equally in need of Christ's redemption and one nation is not in God's eyes more important than another. Yet with limited resources, churches that wish to do more than aimlessly "plow the fields and scatter" are wise to determine priorities. As good stewards, we should study the signs of the times and assign reserve personnel and monies to strengthen the work in areas of particular need or of unusual immediate promise. Christ waited until the time was ripe before making his final challenge to the authorities in Jerusalem. At this moment, these small countries on the rim of Asia are in particular need, in a state of crisis, have an unusual potential contribution to make, are open to the church, and are expectant. Merely to continue routine work at such a time would be irresponsible.

The Christians in East Asia are few. They cannot be expected to save their nations or work miracles of statesmanship, but they are an active, creative minority. By and large, they are better educated than their neighbors, a bit more concerned, more of a community in their common faith, worship, and witness. God may be expecting more of them than we expect. Augustine's faith that the little, struggling Christian communities of his day were an already visible part of the City of God must have seemed ludicrous to his secular contemporaries. God uses "minorities," "remnants," "leaven." Here is a section of the City of God that deserves our attention.

Since our total way of life is affecting their total way of life, then, in all conscience, we must learn all we can about them and all we can from them. Only so can we participate with them in Christ's mission to bring redemptive love to bear upon the inflamed tissues of our ailing world.

✳✳✳ 2 ✳✳✳

INTERRELATED, YET DISTINCT

South Korea, the Ryukyu Islands (including Okinawa), Taiwan, and Hong Kong are scattered, from north to south, over a distance as great as from Washington, D.C. to Havana; and, from east to west, as far as from Ottawa to Minneapolis. The total land area of the four regions is no larger than Michigan; yet, with high mountains and thousands of little islands, many uninhabited, the area contains a population greater than that of Michigan, Wisconsin, the New England states, Hawaii, Alaska, the District of Columbia, and Canada combined.

Why should these four countries, with such diverse histories, be considered together? Even in Asia, there has been little regional consciousness. Only one university in Japan offers credit courses on Korea, its neighbor. In the Philippines there is a beginning of Southeast Asian studies, but little is known about neighbors to the north. Bookstores in Hong Kong have few histories of Taiwan, and in Taiwan's capital city you would be hard pressed to find books on Okinawa or Korea.

The rim of East Asia has been dominated for centuries by big brothers: China, Japan, Russia, and the West. Because of this domination, the people of the region have more in common than their isolation from each other would lead you to suspect. All four countries have been permeated by the competitive and complementary influence of Chinese and Japanese culture. These cultures are complementary because of their common historical origins, mutual indebtedness, and obvious similarities, yet they are different just as the people are different.

Through the centuries the Chinese and the Japanese, as armed powers, as trading peoples, and as carriers of culture, have moved back and forth across these stepping stones between them; now one dominant, now the other. In the shops and museums from Hong Kong to Seoul the objects of art show a family resemblance, a common creative approach, despite intriguing differences. Each one of these areas at some time has been politically subject to either China or Japan, but the cultural debt has been of far longer duration and greater spontaneity.

The whole area still observes the lunar calendar and has common festivals. The Gregorian calendar is official, but the family New Year celebrations are in February and the farmers plant, harvest, and observe the mid-autumn and other festivals according to the moon. Even the Council on Christian Literature for Overseas Chinese, in Hong Kong, prints its annual pocket diary with both lunar and Gregorian dates.

There are linguistic ties throughout the area. From Seoul to Hong Kong, if you can write Chinese characters you can travel without difficulty. If you can speak or read Japanese you can travel easily in Korea, Okinawa, or Taiwan and will not have much trouble in Hong Kong, where you can read the signs (the characters being a part of both languages).

Commercial ties in the area go far back in history. By the second century B.C., Chinese of the Han Dynasty had an overland trade route to Korea. It is not clear when Korean trade with Japan began, though it is known that in the 14th century Yi T'ae-jo selected three ports in the south of Korea for trade with Okinawa and Japan. In the same century Okinawans were engaged in regular trade with China, Japan, the East Indies, Korea, and, by 1409, Siam (Thailand). Taiwan lies squarely in the path of trade routes along the China coast between Southeast Asia and the Ryukyus, Japan, and Korea to the north. Before the Dutch established their trading stations in 1624, Taiwan had already been exporting deer skin, deer meat, sugar, and rice. Hong Kong very early had trade connections with the Yangtse River Valley and Indonesia. From the thirteenth century on, Chinese settlements in or near Hong Kong maintained commercial relations with the south and west, through Arab, Indian, Persian, and Jewish merchants.

These four parts of East Asia have another basic element in common: the Confucian family system and ancestor worship. In the villages, from Korea to Hong Kong, family relationships are surprisingly similar, as are marriage, birth, and funeral customs. In the cities the corrosion of modern, or Western, or even Marxist ideas, is felt, and industrialization has disturbed and changed the family. Elsewhere, filial piety, respect for elders, a ritual for honoring ancestors, concepts of politeness, gratitude, personal obligation to friends, loyalty, and similar qualities retain their Confucian flavor and are the accepted criteria of conduct—in unconscious belief if not always in practice.

Throughout East Asia there are common religious traditions. Buddhism is a pervading influence, though in these four countries it is resurgent only in Taiwan. Traces of a primitive animism are found everywhere, as are Confucian ethics. The Christian church is established and growing in each of these countries. Despite local differences, a traveler feels that he is in a familiar religious setting as he passes from one country to another.

The whole rim of Asia has felt the penetration of the West. Western sailors act the same way in Wan Chai, Hong Kong, as they do in Naha, Okinawa, Keelung, Taiwan, or Pusan, Korea. Western or modern science is taught in all high schools and colleges, and Western medicine is displacing ancient herbal remedies. Western clothes are seen on school children and adults alike. The armies look Western, the airplanes definitely are. The railways are Western. The textile mills look like those in Lancashire, England, or Birmingham, Alabama. Political philosophies are copies or combinations of Western ones, or deviations from them. This penetration by the West has created the same problems everywhere, and

Asian peoples have gone through similar phases in their resistance or acceptance. Early Portuguese and Spanish and
Dutch and British traders pushed at all their ports. Western
missionaries penetrated further inland. The area has a common history with regard to the West.

Today these four countries are involved in the same battle
for the mind. Similar books are found in the different bookstores. Even in the most restricted corners, Marxist books can
be found. Christian bookstores are also present.

Over the whole area hangs a potential avalanche. With the
possible exception of Hong Kong, the region faces almost
identical problems of inflation; of the extension or restriction
of civil rights and democratic procedures, and of freedom of
speech and press; of foreign aid and how to avoid becoming
dependent upon it; of budgets swollen with military expend-
iture; of the explosion of population; and the need for more
and better schools. As you pass from one of these countries to
another, you meet the same issues and feel the same tensions.

Except for Okinawa, each of these countries has an agoniz-
ing refugee problem. It is not only a physical one—how to
feed, clothe, and employ the millions who have come with
nothing in their pockets—it is also a problem of mental and
psychological adjustment. The refugees are not like the local
people. Their food habits and religious and moral customs
are different. Sometimes they are cleverer, stronger, more
aggressive, and displace the local people. Others seem unable, after years, to secure an economic foothold in the new
environment. Churches do not always welcome them. Governments cannot bear all the new burdens or house all the
strangers. Welfare agencies become desperate and turn many
away or employ untrained social workers to deal with the
long waiting lines. Missionaries and pastors make decisions

they are not trained to make; and, with little time for study, prayer, or pastoral work, they become confused and weighed down by the burden of human problems they are asked to solve.

Taiwan and South Korea, particularly, face related problems and dangers with a similarity of outlook. Both have governments that claim sovereignty over larger areas than they effectively control. Both are plagued with the bitterness of recent civil wars. Both are challenged by strong military governments backed by the Communist world and claiming to be the only rightful ones. Both tend to think of and propose solutions to communism in military and political terms only. Both have experienced rule by strong older men who disliked opposition, tended to confuse national and party loyalty, and favored a political orthodoxy in thought and public utterance, deviation from which was dangerous. Both countries went through such a long struggle against imperialism and foreign aggression that they are ill-prepared to turn their attention to the new and subtler dangers of unchecked nationalism. Both have unbalanced economies, are dependent upon foreign aid, and have heavy military organizations beyond the power of their tax structure to support.

Okinawa and Hong Kong are less like the other two areas. Though outwardly having little in common, they show something of a kindred spirit. Both are small in size and do not expect to be independent nations. Both are now rather friendly to strangers. Both are controlled by Western powers but are allowed considerable variation of viewpoint and freedom of expression. In both, the attitude toward communism is less single and rigid; there is more neutralism or third force opinion. Both face problems of shortage of good land, of unemployment, and of pressure to emigrate.

Throughout the area there is a sensitivity to foreign direction; a desire to be aided, but trusted; to dictate the terms of foreign aid, yet keep it coming in ever larger quantities. The use of one nation's resources in another when the receiving nation's livelihood and destiny depend upon such aid is a baffling and tricky business. Were Santa Claus to stay in sight all year he would soon be discredited and ridiculed.

As in postwar Berlin, which is a source of irritation to right and left in Europe, it is to be expected that these buffer states in Asia, these areas between the lines, or eyes at the heart of the typhoons, will be misunderstood and exploited and will most certainly suffer. The church in such areas often is a center of healing and of understanding where men learn more of the meaning and uses of suffering, accepting it as they work to remove its causes.

Can refugees be made into assets? Is it possible that people who have firsthand, frontline experience of the conflicts of our time, who know the intense loyalties and divisions that disturb us, who have survived violently contradictory ways of life and points of view, can lead us toward new solutions we have not thought of? May not the church, weak as it is, yet powerful in its faith and reconciling in its love, and guided by the Lord of History, be again, in such times and places, the creative fellowship, the minority, that turns the thoughts of men from escape or violence to witness, mission, and demonstration of community? Is this wishful thinking or God's command to those who have ears to hear?

KOREA

✳✳✳ 1 ✳✳✳

AN ANCIENT BUT TROUBLED PEOPLE

Koreans are of mixed ancestry. Migrants from northeast
Asia settled the Korean peninsula over a period of thousands
of years. The myth that Koreans are descended from a bear,
turned by the son of the Creator into a human being, sub-
stantiates this early relationship to northern neighbors. Another migration from the south through the Ryukyus also
may have touched the peninsula. Very early, Chinese city-
states with a relatively high civilization made contact with
the tribes huddled in the Korean river valleys. Korean culture combined these Chinese elements with customs derived
from the north.

The heart of the early Korean culture was in the northeast,
along the overland trade routes to China. The Ch'in emperor
(213 B.C.) by burning the books of China, drove many intellectuals into refuge elsewhere and, by building the Great
Wall with forced labor, caused many common people to migrate also. Those who reached northwest Korea overland, or
the southern shores by sea, brought a stimulus similar to
that of the Greek scholars who, after the fall of Constanti-
nople, contributed to the Italian Renaissance.

The Three Kingdoms

Chinese armies, defending the trade routes, attacked northwest Korea in 108 B.C. and the region lost its independence. Soon, however, a Korean dynasty, the Koguryo, set up a capital near the Yalu and became one of the "Three Kingdoms" that long dominated the peninsula.

A state called Paekche expanded from a site near present-day Seoul and became another of the Three Kingdoms. To the southeast, in the area above Pusan where Chinese immigrants had settled, local tribes formed a kingdom that later became known as Silla. Relations between the three kingdoms were often broken by fighting and intrigue. In 415 both Koguryo and Paekche accepted investiture by the emperor of China. This involved mutual obligations and recognition of China's cultural superiority, but no loss of autonomy.

In 660 the Paekche Dynasty came to an end, and in 668 the Koguryo Dynasty was finally destroyed by the Chinese. This left Silla in a position of dominance. She endured attacks by Japanese pirates and by an invading T'ang Dynasty (Chinese) army, but finally defeated both. During Silla's period of greatness, she stressed intellectual and artistic life, developed mineral and agricultural resources, exchanged envoys with Japan, and re-established harmonious relations with China. Finally weakened by luxury and revolts, the kingdom came to an end in 918.

The Koryo Period

The next dynasty, the Koryo, lasted from 918 to 1392 and was the first kingdom truly to unite the entire peninsula. During this period, the Tartars from Manchuria overran part

of Korea several times, but finally agreed to normal diplomatic relations. Buddhism became the state religion and
added to the political confusion and court extravagance, but
it did enrich Korean art and architecture.

In the thirteenth century the Koreans could have allied
themselves with the rising Mongol power already ravishing
China under Genghis Khan, but they were repelled by the
fur clothing of Mongol envoys and by their desire to shake
hands with the Korean king. Relations deteriorated and the
Mongols, looting and raping, drove many Koreans to the sur-
rounding islands. Twice, Kublai Khan involved Korea in unsuccessful expeditions against Japan in which thousands of
men were lost in storms. For fifty years the Mongol occupation brought misery and debauchery, but in 1364 Koryo
troops under General Yi T'ae-jo annihilated a Mongol army,
and the Chinese ended the Mongol scourge in 1368.

While the Mongols had been eating out the heart of
Korea, the Japanese, in raiding groups similar to the Vikings,
disturbed Korean shore villages. These attacks lasted for 150
years. General Yi, proving effective also against these ma-
rauders, was put on the throne in 1392. Envoys were received
from the Ryukyus and Japan, and Japanese trade was regular-
ized.

The Yi Dynasty

The Yi Dynasty stressed the Confucian tradition and improved the lot of the people. During this dynasty, particularly
in the sixteenth century, Korea reached the highest stage of
culture in its history.

In 1591 the Japanese military genius Hideyoshi invited
Korea to join him in conquering China, but the Korean king
rebuked him. In retaliation a Japanese army with European

weapons seized Pusan and quickly overran Seoul and Pyongyang. However, Japan's reinforcing fleet was destroyed, and
the Koreans turned to guerrilla warfare against the invaders.
Finally, a Chinese army arrived, helping the Korean forces to
push the Japanese south. A second Japanese expedition was
turned back by Chinese troops. Korean recovery was slow.
Cities had been looted and burned, and the friendly Chinese
armies were a burden. In 1627 the Manchu, threatening
China, also attacked and laid Korea waste, forcing a brief
recognition of their sovereignty.

These three great invasions, Mongol, Japanese, and Manchu, convinced the Koreans that they should become a her-
mit kingdom, and isolation became the accepted policy. The
last Yi king was removed from his throne by the Japanese in
1910.

Western Influence

In the seventeenth century sailors introduced European
influences that threatened Korean isolation. By the nineteenth century national resistance to outside pressures had
changed to argument about how much contact to allow with
whom. The country's diplomacy suffered from the long attempt to protect Korean culture behind a curtain, while recurring cholera and famine weakened the country internally.

British warships began to call at Korean ports. French
priests entered the country in disguise and were executed
when they refused to leave. One reaction to attempted proselytizing by foreigners was the rise, in 1864, of the nationalistic Tonghak or Eastern Sect (Catholics were called the
Western Sect).

Court opinion seemed equally opposed to relations with
foreign powers and to the Christian religion. In 1866 an

American ship, the "General Sherman," forced its way up one of the rivers; the Koreans killed all those on board, including a British missionary. An American who tried to rob a royal tomb became a celebrated case in Korean history books. French sailors, angered by the execution of French priests, looted and burned, causing more persecution of Christians. An American expedition when fired upon retaliated by capturing five forts and killing hundreds of people before leaving without accomplishing more than the French had. By 1876 the Japanese succeeded in getting a treaty signed, and within ten years others were ratified with the United States, Germany, Great Britain, Russia, and France. The country became a prey to the intrigues of great powers.

The Koreans had one thing in common: they wanted to be left alone. The foreigners had one thing in common: they insisted that Korea enter the family of nations. Westerners wanted her modernized, given effective government, internal security, and freedom for the economic and religious activities they considered essential in a good society. They were primarily interested in trade and religion. The Eastern nations each feared that one of the others would seize Korea and endanger their national security and economic interests. Korea was then what Laos and Cuba have become today.

The Japanese Take Over

Before long Japan and China fought on Korean soil, and when war between Japan and Russia broke out, Korea was forced into alliance with Japan. In 1910 the victorious Japanese incorporated Korea into their empire with British and American diplomatic consent. The Koreans, however, could not see why they should be absorbed into a culture they did not consider superior. They resisted.

The Japanese hid from the outside world their savage suppression of continuing resistance, reporting instead the great accomplishments of the new regime. They stabilized the currency, raised the national income, modernized transportation, encouraged industry and trade, improved agriculture, forestry, medicine, and public health, and reorganized the school system. The separation of education and religion was stressed but not enforced at once, lest useful mission schools close. At the time of the annexation there were 80,000 Catholics and 360,000 Protestants in Korea.

Everything seemed to be going smoothly. Suddenly, on March 1, 1919, thirty-three prominent citizens published a proclamation of independence, sending a copy to the Governor General. They called the police, explained their action, and awaited arrest. Crowds cheered them as they were taken to prison. The proclamation was read publicly all over Korea. The pastor of the largest Korean church, a signer, came down from Pyongyang and joined the others in prison. Of the thirty-three who signed, fifteen belonged to the Chondokyo, which continued the Eastern Sect mentioned earlier, fifteen were Christian, and three were Buddhist. Peaceful demonstrations started all over Korea, and a newssheet appeared daily. There was no rioting, though thousands paraded. It was an extraordinary example of passive resistance to foreign domination.

The Japanese were outraged that a people who had been selected for political and social salvation should want to reject it. Jails were filled and entire villages, including churches, were burned. Christians were singled out because of their democratic ideas, and Chondokyo members because of their intense nationalism.

Opposition crystallized, and independence movements

merged and elected Dr. Syngman Rhee as president, but they were unsuccessful in getting their case before the Paris Peace Conference. Power shifted to the Communists as the early leadership drawn from religious groups was annihilated. The movement was forced underground by the Japanese and under pressure began to split up. Leaders among the escapees in Hawaii, the United States, and China sought democratic support, while those in Manchuria and Russia secured aid under Communist direction. The movement on the left became known as the "Northwind"; the Christians developed a countermovement. Thus two major political groups developed, aligned with the conflicting ideals of the U.S.S.R. and the U.S.A.

From 1920 on, the Japanese introduced reforms and the situation improved somewhat. They further extended primary school education and fostered respect for national treasures and Korean aesthetic values. They introduced new skills in agriculture, but absentee landlords increased their holdings. By 1928 one-fourth of the land in south Korea was owned by Japanese. Forestry policies were destructive. After Pearl Harbor, Korea was stripped of metal, even that in musical instruments.

Divided Korea

At the end of the second world war, the Koreans found their country divided by a decision of the victors. The later history is well-known. It was unfortunate that America was thrown into the center of decision-making in Asia at a time when her education was still provincial. Americans influence the destiny of millions along the rim of Asia, yet American schools usually emphasize European or American history, giving scant attention to other parts of the world.

Korea owes much to both China and Japan, though her people are as different from both as the Irish are from the English. Intensely independent by nature, the Koreans want to borrow only the things they choose to borrow. Unfortunately, nature placed them like iron filings between two great magnets. One can sense their frustration and desperate inner struggle for unity and permanence of culture and outlook. No wonder Koreans grasp eagerly for unyielding orthodoxies and strike out, even in church, at those who deviate from the chosen center of loyalty.

Before the West came actively into the picture, the Koreans were drawn in their religion, philosophy, and art toward the great Chinese lodestone on the continent. The Japanese contributed, more forcibly, much that Korea has learned of modern political, social, and economic organization. If the bitterness fades, the Koreans will realize how much they owe to their island neighbors and how closely their economic destiny must be tied with Japan's. But today the schizophrenia remains, further complicated by new aggressive ideologies and an artificial wall.

✳✳✳ 2 ✳✳✳

GEOGRAPHY AND CULTURE

The Korean peninsula, like a silkworm with its back to the Sea of Japan and its legs in the Yellow Sea, firmly grasps the edge of the Manchurian leaf, and nibbles close to the U.S.S.R. Mountain ranges run from north to south where the backbone of the silkworm would be if it had one. Other ranges extend toward the Yellow Sea in the west, forming the many legs. It is a beautiful land of green fields, and gray thatched villages huddled against sharply rising hills, with dusty-white roads winding beside the streams. The sea to the east is deep, with few islands, few beaches, and few harbors. The tides are low, with a range of two or three feet. On the west coast, the sea is shallow, the islands many, and the tides difficult for shipping, with a range of up to thirty feet.

There are so many mountains in Korea that only one-fifth of the land can be cultivated. The people living in the river basins are cut off from each other by the rough terrain and often live differently from their near neighbors. Foreign armies have struck many heartbreak hills as they tried to push through the peninsula.

Korean weather is like the temperament of the people—fluctuating, subject to storms, given to extremes. The summers are humid and hot, the winters cold and severe. In the summer rainy season, too much falls too quickly, flooding the streams, eroding the hillsides, turning the country roads into seas of mud. Occasionally the rains are too little or too late, and crops fail. Summer storms are noisy with thunder, and passing cyclones hit at any season.

Three-quarters of Korea is classified as forest land; not, however, all as standing trees. Wars, fires, and fuel-gathering have made inroads. The main forest and mineral resources, as well as industrial developments and hydroelectric plants, are in the north. The south has the large food-producing plains, and two-thirds of the population. That north and south need each other is as obvious as the difficulty of doing anything about it.

One People, One Culture

Despite all obstacles to unity, the Korean people have developed into a single race with a common language and a cultural heritage of which they are rightly proud.

Originally much of the Korean housing was semisubterranean, built to withstand severe cold and wind. Later, the people began to build one-story thatch or tile-roofed houses and heated them with flues underneath the floor (an excellent system claimed to have been invented about A.D. 500). The bedrooms are kept warm at night, without danger from smoke or gases, with the families sleeping on the warm, paper-covered floors.

Much early travel was on the small horses that were also the source of the hair for the distinctive black hats worn by Korean men. The originator of this headgear is supposed to have thought that the huge, fragile hats would mean less brawling, always a special temptation for Koreans. The size was later modified more than the nature.

Except for the hats, white has long been the prevailing color for adult wear. This use of white clothing in the seasonal mud of Korea, along with an almost compulsive love for clean clothes, have provided an unresolved contradiction in the Korean character.

From earliest times the Koreans have been fond of drinking, dancing, and singing. The first woman ruler, in the seventh century, sponsored tea drinking as a substitute for alcohol, and shortage of grain in the fifteenth century introduced prohibition of alcoholic drinks. For part of the eighteenth century there was prohibition on moral grounds.

Both sexes dance in Korea, but not together. The folk dances are based on drum rhythms and are not portrayals of historic events. Some are exorcist and related to shamanism, some are Buddhist temple dances, some are harvest dances, while others are purely acrobatic.

Music reached a sophisticated stage by the middle of the sixth century. Lutes, harps, flageolets, flutes, orphic pipes, and drums were in use. Korea also excelled in bell casting. Farmers sang on their way to the fields, and girl entertainers were always popular.

Little early Korean painting has been preserved, but some tomb murals are superb. Stone sculpture outranks the painting. In ceramics the Koreans have been outstanding. During the invasions of the sixteenth century, many of Korea's ceramists were taken to Japan, where their impact is still aesthetically alive.

Solar eclipses were noted in Korea as early as 722 B.C. and sunspots were recorded long before Galileo. In A.D. 789 the Chinese examination system was introduced and scholarship became the road to public life. Korean books, using Chinese characters in movable metallic type, were printed before the Gutenberg Bible. In 1443 the phonetic alphabet, *hangul*, was invented, making widespread literacy possible, though its use was not enforced until Syngman Rhee's time.

Slavery existed intermittently until 1886. Punishments under the penal code were severe and torture was common. But despite the swing between weakness in government and abuses of power, there were evidences of a continuing love of justice and periods of authentic political reform.

Confucianism

The Confucian influence in Korea was early and pervasive. This was not accidental, since there were tendencies in ancient Korea that made the people susceptible to the humane, filial Confucian views.

Early in the Paekche period, Korean scholars introduced the Confucian classics to Japan. After Silla had united Korea, a knowledge of these classics was made compulsory in higher educational institutes. In the Yi Dynasty Confucianism was adopted as the national teaching. In the sixteenth century the neo-Confucianism of Chu Hsi became dominant in Korea, and there was long debate between two famous scholars on the pre-eminence of mind or matter. Other scholars claimed that this abstract discussion lost sight of the true Confucian concern for the welfare of the state and the people. They concentrated on practical problems and welcomed Catholic science and philosophy that gave support to their emphasis. The policy makers of the state, however, remained conservative and persecuted any Christian or foreign tendencies.

Buddhism

Buddhism in Korea has been less sectarian than Chinese or Indian varieties and more of a unifying moral and cultural force. Apparently Buddhist thought provided something Koreans needed, a repudiation of the lust and vainglory of life, a path to virtue and peace, an emphasis on justice and retribution, and fierce devils and vivid hells. Temples were built and sculpture and art encouraged. Later, luxury and power weakened Buddhist influence.

During most of the Yi Dynasty Buddhism was suppressed, though translation of Buddhist scriptures into Korean was permitted. It remained outlawed except for short periods until 1910, when the Japanese annexed Korea.

At the present time Korean Buddhism is larger than it is strong. There are more than 6,700 monks, some 90,000 lay members, and 1,531 temples. Buddhists operate a university, a graduate school, three colleges, and high schools, middle schools, kindergartens, and lecture halls. The temples lost much of their land during the land reform movement, but received compensation that now finances twelve social welfare institutions.

Shamanism

Shamanism with its polytheistic practices remains the greatest single religious influence among the common people. Its animistic beliefs, full of superstition and magic, should recede before Western science, better education and, especially, religious education. However, the subterranean current of the early northern tradition flows beneath the surface. When the Yi Dynasty adopted Confucianism, a gap was left. The people's appetites had been whetted by Buddhist tales of the supernatural, and shamanism moved into the vacuum left by its removal. As late as the nineteen-thirties, reliable reports listed 12,380 professional Korean shamans.

The shamans, usually female, act as mediums, exorcising evil spirits and invoking good ones to provide rain, the birth of a son, family prosperity, or recovery from illness. Other rites express gratitude. The practices are not particularly harmful, but the constant fear of evil spirits and expectation of material benefit from incantations are.

Ancestor worship, also found throughout the area, and thought to be a by-product of Confucianism, is related to this primitive spirit worship. Memorial services for the souls of the ancestors involve three considerations: (1) They provide a regular expression of respect for the departed. (2) They afford the children a dramatization of unbroken family continuity, with its moral lesson of so living as to bring credit upon those from whom their heritage came. (3) They invoke supernatural help for the souls of the departed in the next world. The first two are Confucian. The third, with its fear of the possible return of a neglected ancestor's soul to ruin the family, is not.

Shamanism is slowly passing, and with it divination and

fortunetelling. But in times of anxiety like the present, these aberrations rise from below like weeds from a plowed field. And they rise within the Christian fields as well. This is a danger in both Korea and Okinawa.

Indigenous Cults

A recent book by Korean scholars lists twenty-four new nationalistic or eclectic religious cults, in addition to two or three with a longer history.

The Chondokyo, largest of the older cults, grew out of the Eastern Learning Movement of 1864. It was a reform movement against court corruption and combined Buddhist and Confucian ideas, in opposition to the growing popularity of Catholicism. The people of Korea at that period needed consolation, but the Chondokyo founder believed that Roman Catholics preached a passive acceptance of God and a kingdom of heaven in the next world. He felt that man through self-cultivation could become God and the kingdom could come on earth—in Korea, as soon as man liberated himself from tyranny and injustice. He was convinced that the spiritual consolation offered by the West had to be evaluated in the light of its tendency to exploit Korea economically.

The Chondokyo leader attracted such a following among the masses that he alarmed the Confucian ruling classes. He was executed in 1864, his martyrdom spreading the movement, which continued to grow underground, sometimes erupting in insurrections. In the 1890's, four hundred thousand followers lost their lives. In the 1919 independence movement, the Chondokyo, with Protestant Christians, took the most active part. In North Korea in 1948-50 the movement again became politically active, but was bitterly suppressed by the Communists. In 1955 the Chondokyo claimed to have 235 churches, 9,247 preachers, and a million and a half members.

Christian Aberrations

More powerful than the Chondokyo and more dangerous to the church in Korea are recent Christian aberrations like Elder Bak's movement. Bak Tai-Seon, owner of a precision machine company and elder in a Presbyterian church, began to hold revival services in 1954. He criticized ministers and missionaries and claimed direct inspiration. His sermons were passionate and dramatic, and he combined prayer with massage in a form of faith healing. He sometimes claimed a thousand cures in one meeting.

In 1956 Bak was denounced by the Korean Presbyterian Church, and by the National Christian Council of Korea. It had little effect. With day and night tent meetings, he soon had 303 branches and an estimated two million followers. He built a "Faith Village" for adherents who turned over all their possessions to him, and he promised that residents would not taste death. Newspapers reported secret burials, and the courts finally charged him with serious offenses. He was imprisoned in 1959, but released in 1960.

What accounts for the rise of such sub-Christian movements (there are several of them) that bring discredit upon the main Korean Christian bodies? The answer lies in part in Korea's relative isolation from the give-and-take of Christendom's theological discussion; but there are also sociological reasons.

After the second world war Korea was plagued with ideological confusion and intrigue, political murders, economic uncertainty, cultural upheaval, and population dislocation.

The Christian church, freed of Japanese restraint and blessed with government patronage, flourished, evidencing tremendous enthusiasm and widespread evangelism. When civil war broke out, the Communists killed many pastors and attacked Christian institutions in the north and, later, kidnapped five hundred pastors and leading laymen in the south. Inflation caused moral disintegration. Bodies were tired, tempers on edge; calm, charitable thinking was at a low ebb. Churches split. People, in desperation and with experienced leadership gone, turned to apocalyptic and highly emotional forms of religion. Mystery faiths arose, prophesying the end of the world. Christian revivalism did not escape prevailing nervous tension and moral confusion.

Such tendencies can infiltrate the Christian church anywhere in seemingly spiritual garb. By emphasizing only one aspect of prayer, and by offering shortcuts and quick returns in religion, they can reintroduce magic into a faith that has fought long and valiantly to prune it away. This is particularly true if central Christian doctrines and rites are not clearly understood.

Who can blame those who have suffered as the Korean people have (or as the Jews had at the time of Christ) for wanting immediate benefits from religion: healing, security, peace, wonder-working, and national salvation? To ask them to take up their crosses and follow Him, when they want only to lay down their burdens and be invited to the feasts of the kingdom; to ask them to humbly learn from Him to wash the feet of the disciples, when they long for recognition as heroes; to ask them to deny themselves, when they have for so long been denied by others, forced to suffer, and jailed if they were not patient and meek—this is hard to ask, particularly when Western Christians are prospering.

If people bless the Lord for the sake of his benefits, they will bless the Communists or Elder Bak when greater benefits are promised. The church in Korea, beset with these difficulties, needs the penitent prayer and faithful fellow witness of all other churches.

✳✳✳ 3 ✳✳✳

THE CHURCH—FERVENT BUT DIVIDED

The Christian faith reached Korea in the eighteenth century through Koreans returning from the Chinese court in Peking. Korean scholars had become impatient with the sterility of the prevailing Confucianism and with the gulf between corrupt officials and poverty-stricken peasants. Catholic doctrine and Western science and law, arriving together, offered something fresh and hopeful. In 1777 a group of prominent Confucian scholars gathered regularly in a temple by the river Han to study Christian dogma. Six years later one of them, on a diplomatic mission to Peking, was baptized. With his return to Korea, a Catholic movement began in earnest. The believers petitioned for a priest, and in 1795 a Chinese priest slipped across the Yalu in disguise.

The new religion was persecuted as presumptuous heresy for the idea that a Korean citizen could owe allegiance to God, to Rome, and to the Korean government at the same time. By 1800 there were ten thousand Korean Catholics, but a massacre in the same year killed over three hundred, including the Chinese priest and converts in the royal family. In 1831 Pope Gregory XVI formally established a Korean Roman Catholic Church, asking French missionaries to undertake the work. In 1839 another persecution flared, killing French and Korean priests, chambermaids in the court, and others. The church continued underground, and by 1853 it had grown to twenty thousand. In 1865-68 a persecution took the lives of nine French priests and eight thousand Koreans. After 1872, when Korea began to open her doors, tacit religious toleration began.

In 1910, when the Japanese annexed Korea, the country had sixty-nine Catholic churches and about seventy-five thousand believers. Under the Japanese there were seventy-nine Catholic martyrs, and under the Communists more were added. Today there are 433 clergy and some 417,000 believers.

Introduction and Growth of Protestantism

Protestantism touched Korea in the seventeenth century through Dutch sailors wrecked on Korean shores. They gave a vigorous witness. Two hundred years later another Protestant, the Rev. Charles Gutzlaff of Prussia, landed and preached for forty days. In 1865 the Rev. Robert Thomas of the Church of England arrived, but soon he was driven out. He returned on an American ship, distributed Bibles, preached, and was beheaded after the American crew had been killed. He handed his Bible to a wrestler watching the execution and prayed for him, the wrestler later becoming a devout Christian.

In 1882 a treaty between Korea and the U.S.A. was signed, and on Easter Sunday, 1885, two American missionaries, Henry G. Appenzeller (Methodist) and Horace G. Underwood (Presbyterian), arrived. Soon missionaries from Australia and Canada came, and U.S. Southern Presbyterians, Southern Methodists, and many others. Today there are

5,300 Protestant churches in Korea, with a membership of over a million.

The phenomenal Protestant growth in seventy-seven years was no accident. The timing was fortunate. The people were particularly receptive to the gospel, due to humiliation at Korea's seizure by the Japanese. There was also a messianic longing for freedom and for succor, human or divine. Missionaries sympathized, proclaiming a Messiah who saved and liberated men. If ideas of national liberation became mixed with this, it is not strange; it also happened in Palestine. The Koreans would have responded to any message of comfort and hope. Fortunately, the message they did respond to was the eternal one that involves man in a profound liberation.

The pioneer missionaries gave the church a solid foundation. Korean Christians were asked to assume responsibility for church support, worship, and evangelism. New congregations, according to the widely used Nevius Plan, paid the salary of their evangelists or pastors and raised their own building funds. These emphases, and the example of the missionaries' devoted, persistent preaching despite persecution, combined with the natural Korean independence and combativeness to produce stalwart Christians, unafraid of martyrdom.

Strong habits of prayer, Bible study, and family worship kept the Christians' zealous personal evangelism informed and persuasive. The shared communal life in rural and underprivileged areas at times of unusual expense (births, weddings, funerals) drew many into the church. God's grace and providential activity were thankfully recognized and stressed.

Many found depths in the Christian faith and values

emerging within the Christian community that could serve as roots of new national life. They observed that believers and their children were given Christian education, and that those who learned to read their Bibles became, in turn, the educated men in the rural communities. Protestant church procedures also provided practical experience in the meaning and uses of democracy so that Christians became publicly identified with the movement for liberation, equality, and democratic institutions.

There have been waves in the growth of the church. The peak periods were: 1900-10, when the question of Korea's place in the world was coming to a head; 1930-35, when the Japanese pressed heavily for Shinto worship; and 1945-55, after liberation from Japan and during the Korean civil war when part of the increase was due to the movement south of North Korean Christian refugees.

The largest Protestant bodies are the Presbyterian, Methodist, Holiness (Oriental Missionary Society), Seventh-day Adventist, Salvation Army, and Anglicans. Since the war, Southern Baptists, Assemblies of God, Nazarenes, faith missions, and groups with a particular technique also have entered in great numbers.

Continuing Growth

The methods used today to continue the church's growth include regular pulpit preaching, personal work by laymen and employed workers, and evangelism with special groups such as students, youth, inmates of prisons, industrial workers, and men in the armed forces.

Industrial evangelism is well started, but it is a new emphasis in Korea, as is the armed forces' chaplaincy. In 1960 there were 450 Korean chaplains serving in the R.O.K. army, air force, and navy. This seldom has been permitted in Asia except in Taiwan and Indonesia. The largest religious affiliation *reported* among draftees in Korea is Christian (18 per cent).

Bible study, drastically curtailed by the Japanese in the war years and interrupted by the civil war, is being restored to its central place in the church's life in local congregations, district conferences, and in countless Bible schools and institutes. There are thousands of children in Bible clubs.

Sunday schools, religious education, and youth work are vigorous and effective, partly in response to the churches' devoted services to youth during the war and to the new methods being used. This training is very important as the educational level rises. Sixty per cent of the young people being trained are staying with the church and becoming its adult leaders. In rural areas 90 per cent of those seeking baptism come from the Sunday schools.

Christian literature is effective in the armed forces and in the cities where the literacy rate is higher.

Radio evangelism is increasing in importance. Radio station HLKY in Seoul, with three sub-stations in other cities, and the T.E.A.M. station in Inchon have wide interdenominational support. They broadcast in Korean, Chinese, Russian, and English. The largest segment of the listening public in Seoul is the student group. Thirty-eight per cent of those who own radios there are Christian. The broadcasts are nonpolitical and include music, religious instruction, and worship.

The Korean church's amazing record is due to a combination of all these factors, and others. Yet, no church is perfect. There are things left undone, and conditions that harm the church and retard healthy growth.

Multiplying and Dividing

The earlier unity of viewpoint is less apparent in Korean churches today. The divisiveness found in society appears in the church also. Some Christians say that this is a tragic part of Korean temperament. A few add that recent church divisions developed from differences in North American churches, particularly among Presbyterians. Outside issues and seeds of difference within the missions infected the church. Few think that these involve central theological doctrines. They insist that Korean churches have, from the beginning, been orthodox in belief and are undergoing no change now. A handful of visiting Americans have introduced theological rationalizations into what had been recognized before as a power struggle and as human frailty.

The human frailties include: (1) friction between northern and southern Korean Christians and between country churches and the big city churches of Seoul; (2) a struggle by new men for control of the church organization weakened by Communist removal of trained leadership (intensified by considerations of leftover Japanese church property and American aid); (3) excessive criticism—between those who had not collaborated with the Japanese and those suspected of having done so, between those on different sides of the earlier Shinto question, between those who had reacted differently when the Communists pushed south, and between those who had supported Rhee's government and those who had questioned it.

These factors have been aggravated by the spread of rumors that communism had infiltrated the World Council of Churches and the National Council of the Churches of Christ in the U.S.A.; and that the ecumenical movement (clearly implied in Christ's commands) sought a modernist super-church. No wonder many Korean Christians, who had suffered from communism and did not want the authority of the Bible undermined, were confused, aroused emotionally, and misled.

Funds are being provided from America for those who split away from churches associated with the ecumenical movement. Some Koreans who do not understand the issues understand such an offer. The full blame cannot be laid on outsiders, as war, inflation, occupation, and persecution have weakened moral fiber and strained the quality of Korean patience and forgiveness. The Presbyterians have had by far the most serious divisions: in 1945, in 1950-53, and again in 1959.

No one should minimize the harm done. The splits have not clarified issues or separated the sheep from the goats. Good men on both sides have been confused and distracted from their main task of mission and witness into bypaths of acrimonious debate. The church has been harmed, not only *within* by the sin of division of Christ's body, but *without*, in the lowering of public esteem for the church. Fist fights have occurred in solemn church assemblies and bitter debate in law courts over buildings consecrated as houses of God. It is the leaders, however, who are chiefly involved. Pastors often have merely placed their congregations on one side or the other, with no discussion of the issues.

Any division in South Korea today, in her precarious state, aids her enemies. It can be said that Americans are under the same judgment, for the perpetuation of racial divisions is more harmful to the true interests of the United States than the selling of military secrets would be. The churches continue to grow, however, even if, like the amoeba, it is by division. The denominations in Korea are fewer than in

Japan, and many churches are not in controversy. There is still a wealth of spiritual vitality.

Problems

A major task within the church is the restoration of adequate training for the pastors, members old and new, and church officers. This is a delicate matter. Untried men have been thrust suddenly into new and heavy responsibilities by the killing or kidnapping of veteran leaders. Their immaturity is not their fault, but only reflects their lack of training. The need for prepared leadership is not met either by the postwar tendency of seminaries and Bible schools to admit students too easily. Moreover, impoverished congregations find it difficult to pay for the better trained ministers.

The church's training program is being swiftly rebuilt, but it is difficult to establish satisfactory standards with the leaders themselves handicapped, the war-weary people preferring emotional meetings, and a continuing influx of new inquirers. There is now a tremendous problem of lapsed Christians. It is true that through missionary sharing a church's faith grows, but it grows deeper and richer when there is careful pruning and nurture. It is encouraging that among the lapsed a high proportion return to the church if they have had Sunday school training.

Another problem arises from the relative success of the church. Fifty years ago Christians were disowned and persecuted. Now they are approved. This changed atmosphere tempts people to enter the church for superficial reasons. Koreans reveal a zeal and stubborn loyalty under attack, but not always the same strength of character in a time of prosperity and praise. There is a fear that some chosen as church officers are not reborn Christians, for such an office is a way to honor a man for service or generosity.

The church would be stronger in this time of rapid social change if the pastors could bring under the direction of Christ the new aspects of daily life in which members must make difficult practical decisions. Some pastors think that pure faith is all that is needed, others emphasize the fruit it bears, but few seem to realize that Christian ethics, both personal and social, can be taught. One hears of moral breakdown where church leaders have relied upon authoritarianism and strict discipline. Inadequacy of social vision and responsibility is compounded by a temptation to sinful pride in Korean church growth and purity of doctrine as compared with Asian or Western churches. This pride has been overstimulated by foreign praise from mission boards and visiting Christians, for it is naturally exhilarating for visitors to find a church grown strong through tribulation, with thousands crowding predawn prayer meetings.

The Korean church's heavy responsibility for the distribution of postwar relief has increased its sociological problems and moral temptations. Christians were too quickly put in charge of new institutions, with the handling of large sums of money for which, often, they had little training. Foreign aid poured in from all over the world for any need for which a case could be made. Christians who cared about suffering neighbors and relatives found it easy to make good cases. Padding of numbers in need of food or members of a congregation needing a church roof brought larger amounts of aid, and the whole world knew the need was beyond calculation. In the war it had seemed a patriotic duty at times to lie to occupying authorities or collaborators. In the same way in recent church controversy, untruthful rumors have been spread about opponents. Habits are not quickly sloughed off. Let those who have not been through it be slow in the throwing of stones.

Adverse Western Influences

The Korean church does not say that the presence of Americans has demoralized South Korea, but pastors admit that it has made the church more worldly and that the difference between Christians and non-Christians has become blurred. The movies, hit songs, bars, and magazines portray a wider and looser set of values than those the church has nourished. Our total way of life in the West and, particularly, the cheaper and more commercialized aspects of it, are impinging upon the Korean way of life. The Christian faith is not Western and no nation is Christian, yet a faith cannot easily be separated from the cultural medium in which it is presented. The Koreans respond to Christianity, yet are confused and irritated by many Western practices that are contradictory to Christian teachings. We are deeply and reciprocally involved with the Korean people in the continuing struggle to decide whether or not to let the Lord of all life into the whole of our lives.

Another problem arises from the participation of prominent Christians, Catholic and Protestant, in Korean political life. They should be there, but they are as subject to error as other public officials, and the church, in a minority position, is tempted to attach itself too closely to the political destinies of such men. A public reaction against the church is, therefore, always possible on the grounds that the Christian movement, like Buddhism and Confucianism before it, failed to produce men who could redeem the political and social life of the nation.

If democratic ways lead to irresponsibility and ineffectiveness, Koreans may, with the bitter taste of communism still in their mouths, turn to their own history to foster nationalism and develop a Korean equivalent of Japanese military Shinto. Already there are signs of an emerging cult of Tangun, the mythical founder of the Korean nation. In some places shrines have appeared.

Many students and thoughtful citizens look to the Christian schools for help in these problems. There is need for continuous and responsible political and social thinking among all Koreans. It is critical at a time when Communists in the North continue to analyze the ills of Korea and offer their cures. If there is a vacuum in this field, then communism or its opposite equivalent will certainly fill it.

The two largest Protestant church bodies in Korea are Calvinist and Wesleyan in derivation and, therefore, have clear historical precedents for involvement in the whole of a nation's life, but Japanese restraints caused neglect of this aspect of the church's witness. Those restraints are now removed.

Signs of Promise

Despite weaknesses in the church, there are signs of great promise. One is the confidence of the pastors that God will guide the church through this period, as through its earlier serious crises. They believe the present troubles are not inherent, but temporary effects of recent history. Even in North Korea, churches may be closed but hearts are not, and God will not have left himself without a witness there.

There is encouragement that the church is growing faster than the population, faster among the younger generation than among the older, and fastest in the cities. Roman Catholics increased by 50 per cent between 1949 and 1956; the Protestants even more rapidly. In Seoul thirty years ago there were three hundred thousand people and twelve churches. There are now one and a half million people, and four hundred churches. The city of Andong had eighty churches of one denomination in 1950; in 1959, 296. Probably 7 or 8 per cent of South Korea is Christian now, if Catholic-Protestant totals for communicant members and church attenders are combined. This is ground for the pastors' belief that God has opened the door for the church to win the whole of South Korea.

The fact that Christian laymen of all sorts, including students as well as paid workers, maintain their zeal for evangelism strengthens this hope. One hospital in Taegu has founded 130 new churches or preaching centers. A single congregation in Seoul supports forty evangelists in Korea and a missionary in Thailand. This spirit is evident in the active women's work, and in the church's insistence that missionaries are wanted—mainly for evangelistic work, but some with specialized training—to enrich the total witness.

The Korean church has a sense of mission beyond its borders. It has supported missionaries in China in the past, is now an active part of the East Asia Christian Conference, and exchanges missionaries with Asian neighbors. Women and youth are taking an active part in the regional conferences, teams, and work camps. The pastors are confident that Korean experiences have been preparing the church to make a great contribution to Asia and the world. They insist that now is the time to take advantage of the opportunity. The door is open. Help from abroad should not be decreased at such a moment, but so given that the church is truly strengthened for its great task.

Christian Colleges and Student Work

There are six Christian institutions of higher learning: Yonsei University, Ewha Women's University (one of the world's largest women's universities), and four denominational colleges. There are many Christian secondary schools.

Yonsei and Ewha are more definitely Christian now than they were at the end of the war, due to a deepening of the religious experience of the staff. Ewha's alumni, staff, and students are supporting three Korean missionaries overseas. In both institutions over a half of the faculty and student body are Christian.

The (Southern) Presbyterian College at Taejon admits only Christian students and uses only Christian faculty. Tuition is expensive, but students can work for it, thus breaking the social barrier against using their hands. Many graduates become teachers or ministers. It is church policy in the area to educate Christian youth for leadership rather than to carry on general education. Secondary schools maintain a 60 per cent average of Christian students, often higher. Daily chapel is required, and two hours of Bible study a week.

Formerly most Christian youth attended Christian schools. Now, many are in government universities where they are subjected to varied ideological and religious pressures.

The Y.M.C.A. and Y.W.C.A. were the first to enter the challenging field of student work. The Methodists co-operate closely with them. The Korean Student Christian Movement represents the united program of several denominations, particularly the Presbyterians. The Inter-Varsity Fellowship started Korean work about 1956 and concentrates on schools not organized by the K.S.C.M. The Campus Crusade for Christ carries on personal evangelism among non-Christians. Many other students are served by a Methodist student

group, an Anglican student center, and hostels accepting
Christian students only.

In July 1959 a co-operative council was formed that is recognized by the World Student Christian Federation. Joint
study and leadership training are under way, and awareness
of ecumenicity is growing.

Theological Seminaries

South Korea has more theological graduates per church
member than any other country. There are ten major theological seminaries with over 1,300 students (more than India or Africa) and scores of night seminaries and Bible Institutes. There are churches waiting for the graduates, though
many country chapels use unordained evangelists and rural
elders for financial reasons. Great need exists for theological
literature, as stocks were lost in the war.

The Canadian-related churches maintain two seminaries,
one in Taegu for rural churches, and one in Seoul. Their
seven hundred congregations have four hundred ministers.
The Southern Baptists have a theological seminary near
Taejon, and co-operate with one in Hong Kong in an Asia
Baptist Graduate Seminary Program. The Anglicans have
one seminary serving fifty congregations; only university
graduates are admitted. The Methodists have a seminary in
Seoul and one in Taejon, together serving 1,100 congregations.

Christian Welfare Work

The statement that the Korean church tends to overlook
the new social aspects of the church's redemptive task should
be balanced by a description of the older types of social work
that have been undertaken. From the beginning, medical

and educational work was stressed. Great hospitals like Sever-
ance introduced modern medicine to Korea. The Southern
Presbyterians' hospital in Chunju has made an unusual contribution in nurses' training, standardization of drugs, and
improvement of laws dealing with medical practice, sanitation, and public health. Anglicans use mobile clinics in rural
areas. Education and literacy work is carried on by most of
the church bodies.

The care of orphans has been undertaken by missions,
churches, individuals, the Christian Children's Fund, World
Vision, Inc., Save the Children Fund, Foster Parent Plan,
T.E.A.M., and others, in addition to the government. The
great need now is more vocational training and placement.
Some older children still run away from orphanages to end
up in juvenile gangs or prostitution.

Another immediate need is adequate care of babies abandoned by households where there is severe poverty, one parent dead, or the mother unmarried. In Pusan three or four
babies a day are abandoned, half of them illegitimate.

The Union Christian Service Center near Taejon is a co-
operative effort of United Presbyterians, Southern Presbyterians, Methodists, Salvation Army, and the United Church of
Canada. There is a boys' orphanage related to a Salvation
Army trade school; a Christian Rural Life Institute to train
youth after their army service in better farming methods,
community leadership, public health, and literacy work; an
amputee project sponsored partly by Church World Service
that makes and fits artificial limbs and offers physical and
vocational therapy; a T.B. rest home; and a foundling home.

The Mennonites also have a varied program of relief and
welfare work, vocational education, an agricultural project,
and a hospital advisory service.

Other constructive Christian projects are found, little publicized but of abiding value. Church World Service is aiding many of them.

Despite suspicion of social work as implying a "social gospel," Korean Christians are becoming aware of the urgent need for practical training in this field and for a more educated social conscience in the church.

The Methodists, who introduced modern education to Korea and were involved in medical work from the beginning, have an active Department of Social Affairs in their Korean church. The Catholics have a good school of social work. There are a few others. Recently a Christian Social Research Center has been started in Seoul by theologians and social scientists to bring a Christian perspective to bear upon the causes of Korea's social problems.

The great, permanent need is to save and fully release the capacities of God's children.

✳✳✳ 4 ✳✳✳

THE NEW NATION AND AMERICAN AID

The Korean state, like a tanker torn apart off Cape Hatteras, has the bulk of the crew and the food supplies in one jagged half and the fuel and machinery in the other. South Korea has floundered a bit, but is still afloat and looks as though it will make port. There is rough weather ahead and considerable battening down to do, but if the crew cooperates the half ship can be saved with all aboard. The economic problems are not insurmountable, but they are alarming.

To become self-sufficient, South Korea must meet her power shortage, produce more consumer goods, and secure a better balance in foreign trade. The possibility of developing local hydroelectric power is limited. Thermoelectric power is more practical. There is no oil, but there is an abundant supply of low-grade anthracite coal.

In replacing imports with local products, a good start has been made with chemical fertilizers and rayon, but larger amounts of foreign capital will be needed. At the moment, rice is the main possibility for increasing exports. The Japanese like Korean rice and are willing to pay a premium for it. Trade with Japan has a political aspect. Japanese firms still claim ownership of property in Korea. South Korea might become an appendage of the Japanese economy. Koreans admire and envy but are psychologically afraid of the Japanese; yet the need for a balanced economy is great, and Japanese trade is part of the solution.

South Korea has few commercial minerals. Brass products could be exported, and there is good sand for crystal work and clay for chinaware. There is only one center of heavy industry, near the main coal deposits.

The most serious economic problem is the rural one. The average Korean farmer's yearly income is under ninety dollars, yet some of the consumer goods he uses are imported and expensive. The farmers need larger farm units and a more reliable water supply. Soil conservation and reforestation would help if cheap fuel could be found to replace grass and wood. Only 23 per cent of the land is arable, and each acre must support four persons. The government is reclaiming marginal land and flooded areas along the coast, but hope lies chiefly in improving farming methods.

Inflation, which has so plagued Korea, is being brought under control. In the immediate postwar period prices rose from 50 to 100 per cent a year. In 1957 a stringent financial

stabilization program was introduced and a shift began from
an economy of aid to one of reconstruction. Wartime interest
rates were 10 per cent per *month*, but are now down to 3 or 4
per cent.

In the past direct income taxes were the main source of
Korean tax revenue. Many officials were needed to investigate individual incomes, with consequent temptation to corruption. Taxpayers practiced evasion. Now half of the taxes
are indirect and there is less dodging.

The Human Element

Human factors affect the economic situation. Many business ventures fail because of desire for immediate profit rather
than for satisfied customers. Korean life recently has been
drab. The people who formerly had possessions miss them.
They crave luxury items such as radios, cameras, cars. More
money than is necessary goes into clothing.

Confidence in the future is needed. People are afraid of
long range investments. Trusts or corporations are new. An
investor doubts if he can get his money back unless he is one
of the inner circle, a relative of the owning family, or controls 50 per cent of the stock.

Unemployment is serious. In 1960 one-fourth of the labor
force was unemployed. In the past a man found a job
through family introduction, but the war upset that system.
It is hard to discover what jobs are available.

Before unskilled men can be put to work in industry,
trained personnel for management must be found. The Japanese managerial staff were not retained after the war, except
in North Korea. There are factories lying idle with no one to
run them. Good engineering schools are available, however,
and Washington University, in St. Louis, has a contract with

two Korean universities to teach management skills, so there is hope for improvement in the future.

There are other encouraging signs. Trade is increasing with Japan, and northern refugees are being absorbed into the economy. Some are already prospering. It is surprising how fast the country is rebuilding, despite the scarcity of natural resources and industrial skills and the heavy military burden (50 per cent of the budget). There is also a marked improvement in the average Korean home.

Foreign Aid

Aid must continue because people need food, many are still undernourished; and it must continue until job opportunities are expanded, for there is too much unemployment. It must continue because without help South Korea would succumb from internal dissension and weakness to dictatorship or control by the North. The world picked up Korea's problem and cannot drop it. It is within the concept of a responsible community of nations that help should be given.

South Korea could, with careful planning, feed its own people. But it has to sell part of its food elsewhere in order to employ its workers and pay for the imports necessary for industrialization. The alternative to foreign aid, therefore, is to starve the people. It is bad for any country to depend long on foreign subsidies, however. Decisions about money involve power over lives. Power exerted by foreign interests breeds resentment.

There is also grave danger of making people dependent and of weakening moral fiber through the temptations involved in administering money given by distant donors. Moreover, the equilibrium of a nation is upset by foreign aid. If buses are introduced, immediately repair shops, rubber factories, gasoline stations, lunch counters, road surfacing materials, and other things are needed. A chain reaction is set off that changes habits, affects culture, causes upheaval. The process must be carried forward until a new equilibrium is achieved. In South Korea it will take ten years at least to introduce enough industry and changes in the economy to avoid losing the effect of all the former aid.

Much of the present aid is directed toward helping the Korean people solve their own problems, but the surplus food program contributes least to this. It was essential when the refugees were pouring south, and still is while Korean rice must be sold to help balance the economy. The number in need of direct feeding has dropped to half a million. As refugees find jobs, their places are taken by unsuccessful farmers who move into the city bread lines. When the surplus is eaten, it is gone. The Koreans are alive but no better off. They understand that the food is not wanted or needed in the U.S.A. It is given to individuals rather than to projects, making the people the end points rather than participants in the process. The surplus food program is a godsend in an emergency, helpful in an improving situation, but never a substitute for a long range rehabilitation program.

Effect of Foreign Aid upon the Churches

The foreign aid program, in relation to the churches, has done incalculable good, but it has had harmful effects. The aid was not greater than the need, but it reached Korea in quantity so rapidly that the churches could not work out sound principles and methods of distribution, or find trained personnel for administration. Starved, ill, crowded, or homeless people were everywhere. Decisions had to be made without delay. Compassion had quicker reflexes than intelligence.

Lives were saved and morals were ruined. Self-support in the churches was undermined.

It was difficult to get the relief to the actual need. Casework is a slow process and there were few trained caseworkers. Much of the distribution through the churches, to avoid criticism from the rejected, was by the method of thin and equal spreading. There were some misuses, for inexperienced people were handling large quantities of what their neighbors and relatives desperately wanted. Censure created resentment and division. Power struggles within churches developed because control of relief distribution offered prestige and authority. Some Christians who received goods sold them and contributed the money for church buildings. A desire for the buildings and paraphernalia of religion took precedence over weightier matters of the spirit.

Relief money, food and clothing, in themselves, did not harm Korean Christians. But they often did provide occasions for stumbling. The church can be blamed only for not developing a stronger social conscience, for neglecting ethics in its training program, and for not providing adequate experience in welfare work for its laymen.

Church World Service at first distributed only to churches; then 70 per cent to non-Christians, 30 per cent to Christians; finally, percentages were removed and anyone in need became eligible. Advisory committees were set up, distribution lists made available, and feeding stations established. Every effort has been made to develop a responsible program.

The direct distribution of used clothing is now less needed. If the clothing could be sold before shipping and the money sent to buy Korean textiles, it would encourage local industry, and the materials could be given to widows' projects for the sewing of Korean-type clothing.

The Political Situation

The political prospects in South Korea are soberly optimistic. The April revolution of 1960 showed that the younger generation had courage and concern for the state of the nation. The present period is one of transition. When Syngman Rhee's Liberal party toppled, the Democratic party and unaffiliated officials were unable to keep factions from forming. Action was difficult and lethargy developed. Charges were made of corruption and ineffectiveness. The good men available were not well-known politically and no one figure caught the imagination of the people. The army lost patience and took over, with less democracy but more efficiency.

The present pro-Americanism could turn into anti-Americanism. American servicemen are not under Korean law, and serious incidents could impair relationships. Occasionally students show evidence of anti-Western or anti-Christian attitudes. Regardless of political changes there is likely to be a growth of "Korea for the Koreans" sentiment. Mob rule is still a danger. Schools are often terrorized by student attacks on the curriculum, school officials, the examination system, and strict teachers. These demonstrations provide chances for exploitation by other groups.

Do the South Koreans want a Socialist welfare state? Welfare, yes, but socialism, probably not. If no Communist invasion had occurred there would have been some demand for a Socialist economy. Now it is clear that the people want a free democracy. In the 1960 elections a number of candidates ran on a Social Democratic ticket. Only 3 places out of 230 were won by them and those elected were outspoken anti-Communists. Fisheries, railways, mines, to name a few, are under government control since they were formerly Japanese owned, and Korean businessmen do not have the capital to develop them. The political problem is how to use these state enterprises to the best advantage of the people.

Education

The Korean government is aiming at universal free primary schools. The school system is 85 per cent universal now, but it is not free. The country cannot afford that yet. The plan includes education through junior high school.

Western criticisms of Korean education emphasize that it uses rote learning, with complete dependence upon lectures. The worst offenders are the secondary schools. Other methods may be too expensive, however. About sixty-five colleges and universities turn out a hundred thousand graduates a year. Twenty-five thousand find suitable employment, an imbalance possibly due to overemphasis on liberal arts or on liberal admission policies (to pay the bills and provide teaching jobs). There is no adequate guidance program or study of the relative needs of Korean society. Students are restless because they do not know what to study or prepare for.

Uncertainty and unemployment breed pessimism. The suicide rate is high in the second and third year of high school and the first year of college. Pessimistic movies are common, and popular novels end in cruelty, sorrow, and tragedy. The prospect of a divided Korea, with no solution in sight, depresses the students, as do the grave political and economic problems. They want to move toward Utopia, and are not conscious of the time and patience it takes to build sound institutions. There has been little training in calm reflection or careful planning. Asian students have always had a strong belief that they are the hope of their nations. If their convictions are ignored, emotional upheavals result. The government drafts students for one and one-half years of military service—three years for non-students. This postpones marriage and adds to the strain. However, the drive by students to reform and build Korea is healthy and is influencing the church.

Juvenile Delinquency

The church's work with youth in Korea is important for its own sake, but also because of the serious postwar juvenile delinquency. In June, 1959, eighty thousand juvenile delinquents were known to police and courts. Crowded correctional institutions care for only 2,300 at a time and are not equipped for rehabilitation programs.

Many explanations for the delinquency are given: loss of parents or separation from them and economic insecurity, for example. Three special ones merit attention—the breakdown of moral teaching, freedom after repression, and American example. Korea, originally the most conservative of Asian nations, was thrust suddenly into westernized life. Marriage customs were upset and family ties were broken by the war. Youth, as refugees or soldiers, did things they would never have done at home. Children, without their parents, formed gangs to roam the streets. Koreans discarded the Japanese moral teaching and nothing replaced it except in the more concerned Christian schools.

After liberation from rigid Japanese control, there was unrestricted freedom without experience in setting up the voluntary restraints essential in a democracy. Seats in trains were ripped as a demonstration of freedom of spirit.

At first American servicemen were highly respected, but discipline relaxed. The Koreans had identified morality with nonindulgence in certain pleasures. When thousands of Americans appeared on the streets smoking, drinking, and seeking temporary sex relationships, it was a shock. The image of the West changed. Koreans asked if American standards were falling? Did the church care?

Prostitution has reached alarming proportions and is connected in part with the number of American military personnel in Korea. Many officers deplore this, but do not always see the relation of alcohol to the problem. The men are lonely, homesick, bored, and drink heavily. Girls come to servicemen's clubs on Saturday nights from the villages. A start has been made to meet farm girls on the trains coming into the cities to help them before they get into prostitution.

The orphans of Korea are related to the delinquency problem. Not all are receiving institutional care, and not all the institutions are providing adequate care. Interested friends in America and Canada should give help only through agencies that provide responsible direction.

As a sensitive minority, the Christians of Korea can undertake programs and stimulate public measures that will alleviate the worst conditions. Bernard Kogan in a report, *The Juvenile Delinquency Problem in Korea*, points out that there is not a single trained probation officer in South Korea. He recommends that a comprehensive child welfare law be enacted, with a juvenile court and a separate juvenile police structure; that a shift be made from a purely institutional approach; that suitable personnel be recruited and trained; and that more attention be given to preventive programs, seeking to strengthen family and community life and making use of the many voluntary welfare or religious agencies.

The Future

Overshadowing other problems in the minds of Koreans is that of the future of the nation. Living for years in a state of armed truce is uncomfortable. The ultimate unification of Korea is a national goal and a heartfelt desire. Immediate unification is a political slogan on both sides, used to keep the emergency before the people. The government of South Korea reluctantly rejects armed recovery of the North. They want reunion, but not war to get it. Some say, "If the U.N. can solve the problem, good! Otherwise, we'll wait."

Many would favor a U.N. conducted plebiscite but do not believe that it is possible. The present deadlock has made them realize that their independence and unity are intertwined with the wider question of Soviet-American relations. A few are impatient for action, any action, and all live in fear of sudden attack from the north. There is criticism of America for the Yalta division, and of Theodore Roosevelt's earlier disregard for Korean wishes in the Treaty of Portsmouth (without even receiving the Korean delegation). Waiting for an international change of climate seems to be the only course that is open now. But waiting on an ice floe with a polar bear is not restful even when the bear is asleep. To make creative use of the waiting time, South Korea must out-demonstrate the North. With her growing population, unbalanced economy, limited resources, expensive army, and many human problems, it will not be easy to demonstrate that freedom and democracy have brought dignity, strength, and security to her people.

In addition to demonstration, South Korea must develop a political and social theory if she wishes to persuade the North. As in mission work, example is important but, without the Word, it will not win the world. Penguins communicate little to other creatures by their proper posture and sound behavior. Men want to know what accounts for behavior, what a person lives by and for, what motivates his life, what faith guides his judgment and choices. So Koreans must express simply and clearly what their society stands for and aims to accomplish.

At both these points the Christian church has a responsibility. It is not the task of the organized church to save, in a political sense, any society, but it can train men of integrity, it can transform despair into confident courage, it can nourish the roots of true faith and, through the grace of our Lord Jesus Christ, make available in the common life purity, renewal, hope, and meaning. These gifts clarify motives and give a purpose and soul to the body politic.

OKINAWA AND THE RYUKYUS

*** 1 ***

THE BACKGROUND AND THE PRESENT

Asia has a rim—a chipped one, like a restaurant saucer, but still usable. It serves as a protective sea wall, battered and broken by the storms that roar toward the mainland. Island by island it stretches from Alaska across the Aleutians to Kamchatka, down the Kuriles to Japan, and through the 775 miles of the Ryukyus to Taiwan.

Ryukyu originally meant "Floating Dragon" but a Ming emperor changed the characters to mean "Precious Beads." Like a long earthworm that has been chopped to bits, life is retained in most of the parts, only 25 per cent of the 140 islands being uninhabited. The 1,850 square miles of islands now support more than a million people. That is too many to be fed from the 272,000 acres of arable land, except when harvests are unusually good.

Okinawa is the largest and most important of the Ryuk- yuan islands. It is nearly seventy miles long and an average seven miles in width. Its name means "Rope in the Sea."

The peace treaty of September, 1951, gave the United States a temporary trusteeship of the Ryukyus south of 29° north latitude. In December, 1953, the Amami island group was returned to Japan, with 216,000 population and more than a third of the total area. Military government was replaced in 1950 by USCAR (United States Civil Administration of the Ryukyu Islands), which, in April, 1952, established the present Ryukyu government (subject to the supervision of the civil administrator of USCAR through a liaison office). The chief executive is appointed, but the cities, towns, and villages have locally elected officials.

The Physical Environment

The climate of Okinawa is tempered by the ocean and the Japan Current. Rain falls every month of the year, with heavier rains and higher winds in the summer. Some years as many as forty-five typhoons howl in from the sea. They are frequent during the main growing season, and the beating winds and salt spray damage crops near the coast.

Okinawa has some low mountains, but it is mostly rolling, hilly country with a few sharp escarpments. It is a beautiful land. Where the war has not pulverized the work of centuries, the old rock walls, curved bridges, sheltered villages, and contoured fields show the care that peaceful people have bestowed upon a land they love.

The soil is generally a red clay loam over limestone. The topsoil is thin and there are few valuable minerals. Among the plants is a fragrant lily. In 1950, 1,400,000 of the lily bulbs were available for export. Fruit is not as abundant as in Taiwan, though there are sour oranges, papayas, pineapples, and tasty small bananas. Rice, sugar cane, and sweet potatoes are grown. The beautiful big Okinawan pines, gnarled by the winds, are a wonderful sight where they have escaped bombing and shelling. The *fukygi* trees grow tall, dark, and thin and can be planted close together to make excellent windbreaks and providers of shade for the villages.

The small, thorny sapanwood produces a red dye. Before the war, timber was plentiful. Millions of seedlings have been planted and the people are anxious to make the islands green again.

There are poisonous snakes, particularly the *habu*, a larger cousin of the adder. Of the birds on the islands, the white cranes are the most noticeable, standing quietly in the rice paddies meditating on the shortage of frogs.

The islands are surrounded by colorful coral reefs, treacherous for shipping and like sharp knives to the swimmer.

The People and Their Religion

The original settlers in the Ryukyus came in three streams: one, Malayan or Polynesian, from Indonesia or New Guinea through the Philippines and Taiwan, moving north with the Japan "black brine" current; another from the Manchurian-Mongolian area through Korea and southwards from Japan; and a third, mainly Caucasoid Ainu from Siberia down through Japan.

In one version of an Okinawan creation myth, a supreme god (Lord of Heaven) sent a male and a female god to create islands, trees, rocks, and caves. A heavenly grandson was born, who had five children. The oldest became the king, the second the first noble, the third a farmer, the fourth, the high priestess, and the fifth, a district priestess, or the first *noro*.

Okinawans say that Amaterasu, the Sun Goddess, from whom the Japanese claim descent, made her first appearance on earth in a deep cave on Ie Island (where Ernie Pyle died) and that the first Japanese emperor, Jimmu, began his northeastward conquest of Japan from the same island.

In the religious observances, thanksgiving is a prominent

feature. There is no idol worship, but there is a high conception of God as provider of the necessities of life. Stones are always found on the altars, and the closing sentence of the ritual prayer asks God to hear the prayer "through" the stones, but prayer is never addressed to the stones. Incense may be used, paper is burned, and rice and wine offered. Thus fire, food, and drink, the things essential to existence, are remembered in worship.

The bringing of fire is connected with the earliest stories. A daughter of each household conserved it as a communal treasure, a living thing. The fire custodian was expected to remain a virgin and have close communication with the ancestors from whom the fire came. This continuity of the fire came to represent blood relationship and family continuity. The custodian of the fire on the oldest hearth in the community assumed official distinction, her office as *noro* becoming hereditary, passing to a daughter of her brother. Since fire in ancient times was made by striking stones together, the stones, through association, became sacred. The prestige and power of the *noro* helped to give status to women in the Ryukyus. The cult was made the state religion to create a unifying bond in the islands. A seventeenth century king, however, decided that the priestesses had too much authority, were conservative and antiforeign, so he deprived them of their hereditary lands and independence.

Taoism came from China and brought its version of ancestor worship. The practices strengthen family bonds, though the strongest motive may be the desire for worldly success due to support given to the ancestral spirits.

Later, Confucianism, Buddhism, and Shinto became thinly mixed with the family worship. The Ryukyuans think of man as having a godlike origin in which each generation shares.

The body disintegrates at death; the soul enters the hereafter and divides, part merging with God and part becoming reincarnate after seven generations in selected descendants. Death, therefore, is not considered a termination and is not particularly dreaded.

Buddhism entered the Ryukyus in the late thirteenth century through the shipwrecking of a Japanese priest. It helped to introduce arts, crafts, Japanese language, and learning. Although a few temples were built by kings, Buddhism in Okinawa never secured the popular emotional response that it met in Japan. The Japanese permitted only the mystical sects, Zen and Shingon, to work in the Ryukyus. Neither one was suited to the unspeculative Okinawans.

Shinto, with its feeling of awe toward natural forces, easily fitted into and elaborated the Okinawans' simple thoughts about nature. Its influence began to be felt at the close of the fourteenth century, and it was strengthened after the Japanese invasion of 1609. It did not supplant but reinforced Buddhist influence. Shinto stressed love of country, loyalty, and the unbroken immortality of the race; Buddhism, a calm trust in fate and stoic composure in the face of danger and death. Some claim that Shinto was never accepted in Okinawa as anything more than recognition of Japanese overlordship, but until 1945 its ceremonies took precedence over Buddhist, Christian, or local rites.

Confucianism had considerable influence upon Ryukyuan thinking. In the fourteenth century the Ming Dynasty sent thirty-six Chinese families from Foochow to reside in a suburb of Naha. They taught the construction of junks and explained Confucian thought. Later, temples were built, Confucian festivals were observed, a Confucian school was started, and twice a year community sacrifices were offered.

Early History

Early Chinese histories refer to the Eastern Sea Islands (the Ryukyus or Formosa). Taoists had associated the secrets of immortality and of turning baser metals into gold with these islands. In 607 a Chinese emperor sent an expedition to find them. It failed, but in 608 a second one reached the islands. It found no secrets, but acknowledgment of Chinese rule was refused, so captives were taken to China. In 616 or 617 the Japanese record contact with Ryukyuan people, and expeditions reached the northern Ryukyus in 697 and Okinawa in 743, but neither the Chinese nor the Japanese effected a permanent contact. The Ryukyus were independent.

Later Japanese claims to sovereignty rest upon the possible visit to Okinawa, in 1165 or 1166, of a famous Japanese samurai, Minamoto Tametomo. The Okinawans claim that he married the daughter of a local noble, who bore him a son. The restless warrior later sailed back to Japan with his followers, leaving his mourning wife and a child at what is still called the "Waiting Harbor." The son overcame quarreling nobles and assumed the title of King Shunten. He agreed to a theoretical Japanese jurisdiction over the Ryukyus, though this was not followed up until 1609. During the reign of Shunten's son, writing was introduced with the adoption of forty-seven Japanese phonetic symbols. This simple form of Japanese became the language of Okinawan official documents.

In 1260 the Shunten Dynasty came to an end and King Eiso assumed the throne, introducing clear land markings and a regular taxation system. The thirteenth century was one of unusual natural disasters in Asia and in Europe. Eiso's storehouses for grain and arms provided needed reserves for the famine years.

During the reign of Eiso's son, Okinawa was broken into

northern, central, and southern kingdoms that continued from 1314 to 1429.

A strong figure emerged in the central kingdom in 1349, King Satto. He established close ties with China that were to last for five hundred years. Satto acknowledged Chinese supremacy and sent regular representatives to the Chinese court with tribute. From 1400 on, each new Okinawan king was formally invested by an official appointed by the Chinese emperor, and Chinese decrees were read when Okinawan royal dead were laid away. The Foochow dialect became the spoken language of the court. Okinawan trade throughout Southeast Asia spread rapidly. Tribute ships landing at Foochow conducted so much business on the side that the Okinawans many times asked the Chinese court to be allowed to increase their tribute and send more ships.

Okinawan ships plied the waters of Siam, Sumatra, Java, the Malay States, Indochina, Japan, and Korea and were in contact with ships from Portugal, Spain, Holland, and India. Naha became an international city and prospered. The three kingdoms were reunited.

The Japanese court, now growing weak and poverty-stricken, determined to supervise Okinawan shipping and secure tribute. This decision began a rivalry with China for control of the Ryukyuan trade. In 1451 the Okinawans, wanting harmony, began to pay dual tribute and acknowledge two overlordships. When a Chinese envoy arrived, Okinawan officials dressed in Chinese style. When a Japanese envoy came, they changed into Japanese clothes.

The Okinawans received and profited from both civilizations, while the kingdom's economy was supported by sea commerce. Gradually, Japanese pirates and armed European ships destroyed the Okinawan trade.

In 1609 the northern Ryukyus were made a permanent part of Japan's Satsuma territory, and the central and southern islands, though nominally independent, also were controlled by Japanese representatives. Until 1878, however, the Ryukyuan kingdom continued its acknowledgment of vassalage to both China and Satsuma.

Okinawan rulers were usually moderate and democratic. There has been no history of aggression from these islands. Okinawan kings provided the people with weapons when needed. One king in the thirteenth century provided agricultural tools, instead, which so pleased the farmers that he became stronger than the rival kings to the north and south. In the early seventeenth century sweet potatoes and sugar cane were introduced from China and became the mainstays of the agricultural economy. There was no private ownership of land until the 1893-1903 land reforms.

Contact with the West

The nineteenth century saw an increasing number of Dutch, British, French, and American ships entering Ryukyuan waters, all proving that the island junks were now inferior. Naval parties, traders, and missionaries also passed through. Admiral Perry landed in 1853 and 1854, apparently hoping to make Okinawa a center for American Far East trade and political influence (until greater possibilities developed in Japan). All of this worried the Japanese. They increased the garrison, and began to buy arms and machinery from the Europeans.

In 1871 fifty-four Ryukyuans were murdered in Formosa. The Okinawan king appealed to Japan for aid. The Chinese government, in 1874, agreed to pay Japan an indemnity for the families. This suggested that Formosa was Chinese,

whereas the Okinawans were under Japanese protection
China did not object to Japan having primary prerogatives in
Okinawa, but she wished to retain her traditional rights of
tribute and investiture. She appealed to General Ulysses S.
Grant, who was traveling in Asia after retirement from the
presidency of the United States. The Japanese, not wishing
international discussion, acted quickly and made the Ryukyus
a province of Japan (1879).

The Japanese pushed modernization, reorganization of
government, land reform, a new educational system, postal
and telegraph services, vaccination, and new clothing and
hair styles. Ports were enlarged. Emigration was sponsored
and large numbers of Okinawans moved to the sugar planta-
tions of Hawaii, to Japanese-mandated islands, South America, and Japan. From an isolated island people they again
became one of the most widely traveled and informed people
of the Far East.

In 1945 war hit the islands with unequalled ferocity for
the first time in hundreds of years. The Japanese high command had determined to hold Okinawa. The battle began
on Easter Sunday, 1945, with 1,321 American ships streaming
in with 183,000 assault troops. It was expected to last a
month but dragged on for nearly three. The Japanese lost
110,000 men, and 7,400 captured, over 10,400 airplanes and a
great deal of shipping. Suicidal kamikaze fliers day after day
crashed into American vessels. Landings were made and the
island cut in half. Air raids from both sides were so continual
that sleep was impossible. Those fortunate enough to stay
alive became red-eyed, haggard, unable to co-ordinate. Tanks
became stuck in the bloody mud and the smell of rotting
human flesh filled the nostrils. It was a "no-quarters" struggle on land, sea, and air, and the poor civilians hid wherever

they could, many in caves. Finally the Japanese generals committed suicide. The southern part of the island was a mass of rubble.

One would expect the civilian population and the children to have deep emotional scars, nervous troubles, bitterness, fear, and hatred. Yet, today, the faces are open and friendly. One village, before the battle, decided that the oldest son in each family should kill all parents, brothers and sisters, and then himself. The Japanese had made the Okinawans believe that life in defeat was worse than death. Seven of the elder sons formed a guerilla band in order to die fighting. They were captured alive, however, the village's only survivors. One of them, convinced that the whole military philosophy was wrong, became a Christian, took theological training and is giving his life to save his people. He blames no one for his village tragedy except war and the old misconception of values.

High school girls hid in two caves during the final days of fighting. When Americans shouted at the entrances no one replied. Not knowing what the caves contained, the soldiers used flamethrowers and bombs. Some of the parents, now Christian, say that it was what one should expect in war, but that today, while we have time, we should work through the church for a reconciliation and way of life that would make such things forever impossible.

This unexpected generosity and spirit of forgiveness among Christian Okinawans is an astounding, sobering, and challenging fact that should drive us to our knees in reconsideration of the contrast between Christ's way and ours—our circular, self-defeating ways of building new and greater military bases upon sites still warm with the blood of thousands who died in the old ones.

✳✳✳ 2 ✳✳✳

THE CHURCH

In 1622 Christian sailors from Indonesia or the Philippines
were shipwrecked on Ishigaki Island, where they converted
a few villagers. One of these was burned at the stake by Japanese order for refusing to renounce the faith. In 1636 two
European Dominicans tried to enter Japan through Okinawa
but were beheaded. Two centuries later (1844) a French
warship offered French protection against the British and
landed a Catholic missionary and his Chinese assistant for
language study, with the threat that naval forces would
return for these men. Here was the combination the Japanese
dreaded; priests, demands for trade, military threats, and
diplomacy all in one. Two years later a British naval vessel
delivered to Okinawa the first Protestant missionary, and
soon a French warship brought two more priests. The Catholics left in 1848.

In the eighteen fifties French missionaries arrived again. In
1891 Abbe Ferrier began effective work in Amami Oshima,
where his church and school for girls is still active. In the
nineteen twenties and thirties other Catholic churches were
built, and Canadian Franciscans began their work, but the
Japanese government expelled all the missionaries from the
Ryukyus in 1934.

The first Protestant missionary, Dr. Bernard Jean Bettelheim, was a colorful and controversial figure from a prominent Hungarian family. He wanted to be a rabbi, but studied
medicine in Italy, became chief surgeon on an Egyptian war
vessel, later head surgeon for a regiment in Turkey, and was

baptized by an Anglican missionary in Smyrna. He moved to London and was sent by the "Loo Choo Naval Mission" to Okinawa as a medical missionary. He arrived in 1846 with his wife, two children, a governess (who returned on the same ship), and several dogs. Local officials refused to let the party land but they got ashore by ruse. They slept overnight in a Buddhist temple that the monks temporarily vacated. Dr. Bettelheim did not move out, but held the temple as his residence for eight years. No Okinawan was permitted to sell food to the family, so he and his wife took what they needed in the market and left their own estimation of the value. Guards watched his activities and drove people away when he tried to preach to them. He was so zealous that when homes closed to him he would slip over back fences and go in anyway. His offers to teach English, geography, or astronomy, or practice medicine were all refused. Officials begged visiting ships to take him away, but he would not go.

Bettelheim translated Luke, John, Acts, Romans, and some prayers. In his eight years on the island there was one convert, who was soon confined and died in prison. In 1854 when Commodore Perry left the islands the authorities requested that, "to show compassion on our little country, you will take away . . . Bettelheim and Moreton." (Moreton had arrived as Bettelheim's successor.) As Bettelheim prepared to leave he was handed by the government all the coins he had left in the markets for food as well as his tracts that officials had collected from the people.

Missionary Efforts

Missionaries of the Methodist Church began work in Okinawa in 1887 and baptized their first convert in 1891. They were joined later by the Home Missionary Society of the

Japan Methodist Church. A succession of Japanese and American missionaries followed, though from 1926 to 1950 there were no Methodist missionaries from the West in residence in Okinawa.

Baptist work began in 1891 with the arrival of two Japanese evangelists. They were supervised by a Scotsman, the Rev. Robert A. Thomas, and financed by a Presbyterian woman from Glasgow. American Baptists soon sent missionaries to join the Japanese and Okinawan workers. Here was early ecumenical co-operation.

The Church Missionary Society sent an Anglican evangelist in 1898. Soon Presbyterian, Congregational, and Holiness churches were also established. The Oriental Missionary Society began work on Amami Island in 1908. In 1912 Protestant influence reached Kikai Island; a church was built on Tokuno, and scattered work began in the other islands. The Salvation Army came in 1917.

Rapid church growth did not occur until the Ryukyuans themselves took responsibility for evangelism. About 1903 a Ryukyuan official who had been converted in Hawaii won an Okinawan primary school principal. This principal was sent to Japan for further study by an Epworth League in Indiana. Upon his return and within a short time, he had won 120 converts. Such a sudden change of religion brought stoning and community resistance, but the incident proved that Okinawan hearts were not permanently closed to the gospel.

When the second world war began there were a dozen church buildings in Okinawa and eight hundred Christians. The war destroyed ten of the buildings and badly damaged the other two. Okinawan Protestants were merged into the life of the United Church of Christ in Japan; but over half of the Christians died in the war, and all the pastors but one were scattered to Japan or killed. Church organization collapsed and there was no financial support.

In 1945 Christian Okinawans invited missionaries to return, and the U.S. military government opened the doors on September 1, 1947. Within twenty-four hours two Roman Catholic missionaries arrived. Churches were rebuilt in the outlying islands, and work was begun on Okinawa with a laundry, tailor shop and sewing school for war widows, a chapel, a library, university teaching and a student dormitory, a large church, a language school, theological training, medical work, a kindergarten, and a growing Okinawan sisterhood.

It was a year before any Protestant missionaries appeared. The first was a former army chaplain representing the Disciples of Christ. His work in northern Okinawa stressed evangelism and Bible training and resulted in 1,200 members in five related churches.

In 1948 the Methodists sent a husband and wife team to work with Christians who wanted to establish a United Church of Christ of Okinawa. A year later they were joined by another family. In 1950-51 chaplains and servicemen, with their own contributions and gifts from overseas, rebuilt nine churches for Okinawan congregations. More have been undertaken since, most of them related to the United Church.

In 1950 Episcopal missionaries from America arrived. There are now seven Episcopal congregations, over a thousand communicants, a handicraft project producing beautifully designed Okinawan products, an educational program, student work, and a special ministry to the thousand lepers of the Airakuen colony.

Seventh-day Adventist work began in Okinawa in 1950 with both American and Japanese missionaries. They have four organized churches, a membership of four hundred, a radio and correspondence program, schools, and a busy hospital.

A beautiful new Baptist church in Naha stands out against the skyline. The American Baptist Foreign Mission Society and the Japan Baptist Convention work with the Okinawa Baptist Association, which now has fourteen churches or preaching centers and a membership of six hundred. Their work includes kindergartens, a bookstore, radio programming, a monthly newspaper, student work, a Bible Institute, and correspondence courses.

The Holiness Church in Okinawa, started fifty years ago by the Japanese, has a fine church building and two preaching places, with about sixty members and fifty seekers. The church was built largely with Okinawan gifts (earrings, a widow's funeral gifts, retirement money, and similar funds), and the pastor's salary is provided entirely by the tithing of members. They have no Western missionaries, but would welcome one.

After the war, Youth for Christ, the Four Square Gospel, the Orient Crusade, the Far East Gospel Crusade, the Mormons, Jehovah's Witnesses, and other small groups moved in with vigorous evangelism and confusing diversity.

United Effort

In 1945 the United Church of Christ, formed largely by government pressure from Japan during the war, was replaced by a voluntary Okinawa Christian Association. Out of this grew the United Church of Christ of Okinawa, which includes work sponsored by Methodist, Disciples, Evangelical and Reformed, Congregational, and other mission bodies. The first moderator, the Rev. Yoshio Higa, had studied in

America on a Methodist scholarship. After his return to Okinawa he was supported by the National Baptist Board of Missions, a Negro church body. This is a fine example of inter-church and interracial co-operation.

When the United Church sent out appeals for missionaries without denominational labels, the Methodists in the U.S.A. and the Philippines, the Disciples of Christ, and the American Board of Commissioners responded with Japanese, Filipino, and American workers. The United Presbyterians, the Reformed Church, and the United Church of Canada have contributed money but have not sent missionaries. There is an Okinawan Inter-Board Committee in New York, and a Council of Cooperation in Okinawa that determines the use of funds. The United Church has 19 congregations, 18 pastors, 33 preaching stations, 2,000 members and 2,500 children in Sunday schools. In its wider ministry it has a two-year junior college, a student center at the university, kindergartens, an orphanage, a widows' home, a conference campground, two clinics, a mobile medical unit, and a rural center in the Yaeyama islands.

The women's societies of the United Church have seven hundred active members. Religion has always been close to the hearts of Ryukyuan women, perhaps because their men are so often out in dangerous typhoons, and because of the early importance of women in religious observances.

A succession of students have been sent to Japan for theological training, financed by the co-operating mission boards and by servicemen attending the army, marine, and air force chapels. These servicemen also supply much of the literature used in the United Church Sunday schools.

An Okinawa Christian Council brings into co-operation eight Protestant bodies. The Council has many departments, but too small a budget. It has studied the total needs of the people and its requests for help deserve a wide hearing.

There are over a hundred missionaries in the Ryukyus, seventy or eighty Okinawan pastors, and several Japanese co-workers.

The Christian Children's Fund is active and supports the largest Christian orphanage in the islands.

Church World Service forms the nucleus of the Social Welfare Committee of the Okinawa Christian Council. Its work is closely related to the local churches. Relief has been the major work but there is increasing emphasis on rehabilitation: scholarships for blind students; aid to the Episcopal-sponsored handicraft program; marketing Ryukyuan dolls made by handicapped people; and a cattle and citrus fruit project in the hills, developed in co-operation with the United Church. Surplus commodities are distributed under the direction of the welfare department of the Ryukyuan government through a committee composed of church and government representatives.

There are six broadcasting stations, some using both English and Japanese language programs. Rural people are able to listen to broadcasts through a central radio receiver located in each village. The Far East Broadcasting Company covers a 1,200 mile radius with its Christian program. It supplies the microphones, but the main programs are produced by local churches or brought from Japan. Although the total effect on non-Christians is unassessed, these broadcasts are a strengthening influence within the Christian community. The Lutherans also have an hour on the Japanese commercial radio.

The Japan and the American Bible Societies co-operate with the Christian Council in book and Bible sales.

The Lutheran Service Commission of the National Lutheran Council and the Missouri Synod have an inspiring chapel and friendly center serving three thousand military personnel a month, and the Ministry to American Servicemen in the Far East maintains another such center near three large camps of U.S. marines.

Problems

The co-operative spirit and outlook in Okinawan Christian work is good, yet the over-all Christian growth is slow. Many Christian leaders died in the war. The Okinawan churches are poor. The clergy are underpaid and usually receive only a small cash grant upon retirement.

Until recently Okinawan churches had opened few schools except kindergartens. There is good Sunday school work and an eager response from children, but a gap in educational outreach exists between the Sunday school classes and the adult work. Adolescents are not easily attracted and there is a shortage of trained teachers and teaching materials. Many junior high graduates cannot find places in senior high schools. The government has suggested that churches open high schools, but the churches do not have the budget or personnel for this urgent need.

The government has established the University of the Ryukyus, the first in the island's history. It stands on the imposing site of the old Shuri palace, and should play a central role in the future shaping of Okinawan culture. Many of the teachers are vigorous Christians and outstanding scholars.

A Student Christian Movement is active in the University and there is fine Student Center, but without enough stimulating Christian books. Okinawan students have seen too much of life and death to be interested in Christian writing unless it is realistic, honest, and serious. In Japan Christian books are plentiful; more of those that interest students should be made available in Okinawa.

The church is weak in presenting its faith to the general public, particularly to those non-Christians who have the most influence on the island's thinking. An atheist tendency is evident among youth, due to the amazing progress of natural science, exposure to Western materialism, and the influence of Marxist thinking. All religions are thought to be relics of an older age, destined to disappear as time passes.

Ancestor worship persists stubbornly. The pastors consider it, with its polytheistic tendencies, the greatest problem the church faces. Rural evangelism is slow because old customs are retained in the country districts; also because the farmers think of Christianity as the religion of those who took their farm land for the airbases.

The subtlest danger to the church may come not from the older religions but from the secularism of the present age; the temptation to an easy acceptance of the standards of the Western business and military community, or a rigid rejection of them in terms of an otherworldliness alien to the biblical view. God so loved *this world* that he sent his son into it, to save men not *out* of their situations but *in* them. His truth judges equally our excesses of tolerance and rejection.

The church in Okinawa is optimistic. It is now led by Okinawan pastors, with others being well trained for the future. The response to evangelism is better than in Japan, but many Christians leave the island.

The West in the East

Despite the excellent work of the American chaplains and Christian service centers, the ways of the average serviceman do not attract the Okinawan to the faith the Westerner is presumed to hold. Outside of the beautifully kept military camps and airbases—like country clubs with their rolling lawns, theaters, gymnasiums, hobby clubs, and swimming pools—there are acres of dance halls, bars, gambling joints, pawnshops, and houses of prostitution. These were not built by the Americans, but they are there because the men want more kicks than they can get in the clean, supervised social facilities of the bases.

For every Okinawan accepting Jesus Christ there is at least one Okinawan girl living with a serviceman. On an average, one American a day marries an Okinawan girl, but many of the marriages fail because no judgment has been used except Hollywood's. Okinawans dislike mixed marriages, and the wives may find themselves ostracized, though there is greater resentment against temporary relationships. Families care for the children and are willing to adopt them. In the schools the Eurasian children face some discrimination.

Prostitution is open but not legal. In the cabaret area there has been fighting between Negro and white servicemen, but little between Westerners and Okinawans. However, the area has a demoralizing effect upon the community. The relation between alcoholism and prostitution is as clear in Okinawa as in Korea. The Okinawans already had a problem with their own alcoholics, who consume quantities of sake. Drunkenness is used as a shield for crime, light sentences being given if the criminal can prove he was drunk at the time. There is one Ryukyuan Temperance Society (Seventh-day Adventist) and a magazine on the subject, called *Alert*.

No one except God, their pastors, families, and friends, expects large numbers of men, single or separated from their wives, to behave as morally in a strange land as they do in their home communities. Perhaps they live at home with the same disregard for the Ten Commandments and the Golden Rule, but it is more obvious and destructive of human relations in someone else's country.

The situation has improved since 1949 when, in six months, American servicemen murdered twenty-nine Ryukyuans, raped eighteen, and assaulted and robbed forty-nine. The Okinawans have shown unusual understanding of the situation. However, if two foreign armies fought over areas of the United States or Canada and the victorious one stayed on and indulged in occasional murder, rape, and robbery, we would expect resentment among the residents. This would not be eradicated by the efforts of others of the same nationality to share with the local people the religion of the foreign army.

The churches in America and in Asia must deal with this old dilemma in its frightening new dimensions as an urgent task. If they work together to reach the delinquent American and Okinawan, they make a truer witness and double their chances of redeeming the troubled relationship. Asian Christians will hesitate less to speak to Westerners about the Christian faith if they know that Western churches hope they will include in their evangelism and worship the Western citizens in their midst. There are language problems, of course, and Asian churches cannot neglect their other responsibilities, but we in the West can urge our Christian nationals in secular work abroad to do the major part of the work in partnership with them. The Japanese church is doing a pioneer work in this field, which can be used as a guide elsewhere in Asia.

How far is any church responsible for the behavior of its country's citizens overseas? Are you personally concerned when the massive demonstration of American license in the streets attracts the Asian's attention more frequently than does the liberating Word preached within church walls?

*** 3 ***

WHAT OF THE PEOPLE?

Okinawans are a pleasant, peaceful, tolerant group, short and stocky, with more beard than the Japanese. Curly hair is seen everywhere. Although many of their social customs are Japanese, there is a difference—a greater frankness, less reticence with strangers, more immediately expressive faces. They are a singing, dancing people with many lullabies and working and fishing songs. Their drama is largely dance and comedy; love triangle situations are considered funny. The women dance short ballads, taking sometimes a female part, sometimes a male part. There are two types: court dances in which the motions are slow and dignified, and popular ones with a quicker tempo and more action. The movements of the feet as well as the arms and torso are simple, restrained and graceful, and the music is appealing to the Western ear.

The Okinawans seem to be healthy, sturdy, not noticeably undernourished. Certainly, the level of food is better since World War II. It is difficult, however, to obtain an adequate supply of good vegetables and fruit. Despite their healthy looks, twenty thousand are known to have active tuberculosis and there are hospital beds for only six hundred. Eight thousand cases are being treated at home. The government provides the medicine and maintains five health centers. There are 211 doctors in the Ryukyus, eleven of whom are specialists in T.B. Of every thirteen people dying, one is likely to die of old age, two of heart disease, three of nervous or mental diseases, and seven of tuberculosis. There are four mobile T.B. clinics and school children are checked once a year. Help from the West is needed to increase the accommodations for mental and T.B. patients. Heart disease is increasing.

Economic Prospects

The economic prospects of Okinawa are not bright. There is a superficial prosperity due to American spending, but Okinawa cannot easily be made self-sufficient. Natural resources for industry are limited. The island can produce only a third of the rice it needs, and there is serious crop damage from typhoons. Much of the best land is under the concrete of highways and airfield runways. However, the use of chemical fertilizers and better control of pests have increased the yield per paddy of rice, and irrigated crops have doubled.

The transportation system is adequate now, particularly in the cities and near the airports; port facilities have been improved.

Okinawa exports cement, iron, glass, flour, veneer wood, beer, rubber shoes, candy, and sugar. Oil has to be imported. It is American policy to move toward a balanced economy, but the problem is in Washington where budgets for Okinawa are often reduced. Local authorities are promoting sugar and pineapple industries and the making of plyboard for export. The former are prospering now only because Japan exempts them from import duty and provides a favorable dollar rate, part of a wooing process, but helpful. Fishing and whaling are being revived commercially. Toys and dolls are sent to America.

The local cloth, made by hand by slow methods, is unusual and beautiful. Craftsmen produce lacquer ware and some interesting pottery, highly valued by collectors. With large quantities of excellent clay available, ceramics could be developed commercially.

The main export from Okinawa is people: thirty thousand to South America, and many to Japan, Hawaii, and other sections of the United States. Still the island is overcrowded. There is unemployment, although fifty thousand people work for the American military authorities. Before the war the economy was the weakest among the Japanese prefectures, so the problem is not new, and today the standard is above that of several of the Japanese prefectures. In 1960, 15 million dollars in land rentals was paid into the economy by the military forces. The Okinawans cannot produce the capital needed to industrialize and develop the island. Private foreign investors are not likely to show interest because Okinawa does not have natural resources or obvious geographic advantages. Therefore, American taxpayers have only one choice before them. They must artificially develop Okinawa's economy with the permanent interests of the Okinawans in mind, or pour relief funds in indefinitely to alleviate the poverty. Otherwise, discontent and political agitation will endanger the military purposes for which the island is held. Americans are going to have to think and think fast, and any solution will be costly.

Until the economy becomes more balanced, there will be need for welfare work. Both Church World Service and Catholic Welfare work through the U.S. civil government and the social welfare section of the Okinawan government. Church distribution has been in the name of the government and with the distribution lists checked by government, though disaster relief from now on will be handled by the churches. Despite clear organizational ties with the Okinawan churches, the local people tend to associate Church World Service not with the Christian faith but only with America. This lessens the danger of filling churches with rice Christians. However, welfare work as from government alone may be thought of in political terms rather than as a free and voluntary expression of sharing and love. Credit is not what the church wants but a spread across national and racial boundaries of the contagion of love, the stimulation in the receiver of a like impulse to share and, ultimately, a recognition of the divine source of the readiness to bear one another's burdens and of our common stewardship under God for the use of all possessions.

The Political Situation

The political situation in Okinawa is naturally related to the economic. There are three major parties. The largest is the Democratic party, related to the Liberal Democratic party in Japan; next, the Social Mass party; and third, the Okinawan People's party. The O.P.P. is a Marxist Socialist party with a policy resemblance to the Japanese Communist party. There seems to be little direct Chinese Communist influence. The O.P.P. has struggled for reunion with Japan. Seven years ago it was popular but the present government defeated it and arrested its leader. Even among moderates who do not agree with him, he is a kind of hero because he spoke out for the Okinawan people. Many of the grievances to which he gave expression have been remedied. The most serious one arose from the American desire to obtain large tracts of good land for military bases. The farmers were given a low rent until agitation brought a reasonable rate based on crop value. However, the food supply is affected and the farmers feel less secure with money than with land. It is doubtful if the farmers have forgotten, understood, or agreed with the necessity for the action. There is a widespread sentiment of neutralism and a strong peace movement.

In work for the military authorities, Okinawans can only rise so far. There are different rates of pay for different nationalities, and this obtains in the civil government as well. The highest rate is for Americans, the next for Filipinos and Japanese, the lowest for Okinawans. The differences are considerable and noticeable. Administrative orders filter down through the same hierarchy. There is considerable resentment toward those in between.

Money is going into Okinawa to build roads, modernize harbors and communications, and generally improve conditions. However, Okinawans see that military considerations are primary. The highway and communication system near and between the military bases is excellent; in the northern rural districts, where poor farmers must get their produce out quickly to the fast growing cities, the roads are terrible. This imbalance is justified on the ground that care of ordinary roads and city streets (they are full of potholes in Naha, the capital) are the responsibility of the Okinawan government, or its municipal and county authorities.

The salary of teachers is a sensitive issue. The teachers were in a somewhat better position under the Japanese than under the Americans. They were honored and respected more. Their salaries today are comparable to earnings in similar professions, but it was a Japanese tradition to pay teachers more than other white-collar workers. The beginning salaries of young teachers in Okinawa look better now than in Japan, but the Japanese provide bonuses, increments, and pensions. Also, in Okinawa prices are 25 per cent higher than in Japan, so the teachers' purchasing power is less. If the teachers become embittered, their attitudes will rub off on their students, and Okinawan youth will be unhappy and troublesome.

Youth and Morals

Sudden changes and inequalities produce moral confusion in sensitive youth. They notice the sharp contrast between poor and newly rich Okinawans, the rich having money to waste and spend on evil things. Political factors affect them morally also. Okinawans are, in a sense, stateless. Whom are they to serve? There is no possibility of an independent Ryukyuan state, and young people feel no loyalty to faraway America. They are emotionally loyal to Japan, but cut off from her. They feel blocked, as though they had encountered an iron grating across a pathway and could see through it, but could not unlock it or climb over it. If more of them could go on into higher education or secure good jobs, it would help.

There is compulsory education to the end of junior high school but too few schools beyond that level. If students cannot study or find the work they want, they easily become delinquent. From fourteen on, for several crucial years, society seems to have little use for them. Young people are leaving the villages for the cities, where they are freed from the restrictions of home life.

Films, Japanese and American, contribute to delinquency, and cultural standards are lowered by cheap American customs introduced without the deeper levels of Western tradition.

The government can do something about the situation by

increasing educational opportunities, developing industry and employment, substituting service to the people for service to the nation (an Okinawan peace corps), explaining and demonstrating the democratic view of life at more and deeper levels, raising the pay and morale of teachers, and concerning itself with the true welfare of the people.

But the government itself cannot turn the tide. Abundance of things will not fill the emptiness of life. The church, strengthened not only with money and personnel but in the relevance of its witness, the incisiveness of its message, and the aiming of its effort, could find entry to the Okinawan heart and speak the life-giving word at this critical moment in Okinawa's history.

The Future

What are the present political hopes of the Okinawans? The majority favor reversion to Japan. They differ as to when. The more radical parties demand it immediately. A great many recommend the returning of the civil government to Japan but the retention of military bases by the United States. A very few hope America will stay permanently. These prophesy that in ten years sentiment will swing in favor of America. Those recommending immediate reversion admit that Okinawa would suffer economically, since American spending is all that keeps the island from a severe depression. Japan could not afford to spend as much. However, they think that other advantages would outweigh the economic hazards. The Okinawans feel themselves to be Japanese and want to participate fully in Japan's political, economic, and cultural life. They would rather get along with less money in order to feel that they belong, have a "nationality" again, and are part of a culture they understand and can give expression to. Teachers and students are those most anxious for reversion to Japan. The basic urge seems to be for status. The Okinawan intellectuals feel now that they are orphans.

The only hazard that some observers see in reversion is the possible growth of communism. When the Amami Islands were returned to Japanese control, the first party to emerge in strength was a Communist one. If the Americans left Okinawa, economic deterioration might invite such a result. Now is the time to start the Ryukyus on a permanent path of recovery so that when large-scale military spending stops, the islands' economic life will not collapse.

The United States has officially recognized the "residual sovereignty" of Japan, so it is committed to returning the Ryukyus at some future date. Probably nothing will be done until Japan introduces the question in the United Nations. American policy toward Japan and toward the Ryukyus cannot be separated. A change of policy toward the one will affect the other. With the present two-government arrangement, there is not a great deal of freedom for political maneuvering, but there is considerable freedom of thought and expression, as, for example in writing and publishing.

If America left the islands, the churches might in the long run be in a healthier condition. The political and military decisions will not be made by the churches, though they have a responsibility to discuss the moral issues involved. American churches can stress the importance of sending good men who understand Asia into the administrative posts in the Ryukyus. (Okinawans say that with a few harmful exceptions, well-balanced and sympathetic men are being sent.) They can urge that military interests not be the only consideration (God help us if genuine friends are less essential than impregnable bases); that sacrifices be made that will lead toward permanent solutions of the local problems; that the handicapped, sick, and unemployed be given adequate care; that, in addition to more educational openings on the island, fellowships for graduate study abroad be provided; and that Western laymen going overseas live in such a way that a positive contribution is made in the areas they visit. Above all, the church can, through preaching, worship, sacraments, and fellowship, strengthen men disturbed by the collapse of half-truths and false gods, and provide a cause to live for and a faith they are willing to die for.

TAIWAN

*** 1 ***

HISTORY AND PRESENT CONDITION

Taiwan, shaped like a green tobacco leaf floating on the Pacific, would more than cover the states of Massachusetts, Rhode Island, and Connecticut. It is sprinkled with an annual rainfall of 101 inches, with places in the north that have three times that much. Windward mountain slopes may get forty inches in twenty-four hours during the typhoons, which means that everything movable sweeps down toward the alluvial plains. The foothills and terraced tablelands are a contractor's paradise, for gravel is everywhere.

The island is still rising, with sharp cliffs to the east and a gradual tilt westward toward the mainland of China, one hundred miles away. Down the island, like the stem of the tobacco leaf, runs a ridge of mountains with ten thousand foot peaks. The bulk of the agricultural land is to the west of this ridge on a wide coastal plain. The warm year-round temperature and plentiful rain provide a growing season that is continuous for most crops. The weather, however, is not always benign. Taiwan, like Okinawa, is in the path of typhoons that cause tremendous loss of life and property.

Sugar cane, tea, bananas, pineapple, oranges, papaya, and watermelons flourish. Acacia and bamboo grow wild and there are more than 1,200 indigenous species of flora as well as plants and trees common to South China or the Philippines. Truly, it is "Formosa," the beautiful.

The Stream of History

Taiwan's early aborigines came from the islands farther south and formed scattered settlements on the coastal plains. By 611 a fierce people, possibly of Malayan stock, arrived and drove these settlers back from the coast. They, in turn, were gradually driven into the mountains by migrations of Chinese. In 1367 the Chinese made the Pescadores, between Taiwan and the mainland, a part of their empire and soon thereafter claimed Taiwan ("Little Liu Ch'iu"). In the sixteenth century the Portuguese noted the island and called it *Ilha Formosa*, but soon the Chinese began to call it Taiwan, or "Terraced Bay."

When the Dutch landed in 1624, they found a population of some thirty thousand. The Dutch built fortresses, developed trade, and brought missionaries. Spaniards, two years later, occupied parts of the north, built forts, and also began missionary work. In 1641 the Spaniards were driven out by the Dutch. In the meantime many Chinese refugees came to Taiwan to escape the Manchus. In 1661 Cheng Ch'eng-kung, or Koxinga, took the island from the Dutch, hoping to use it as a base for the restoration in China of the Ming dynasty and culture. By that time, the population had reached two hundred thousand. Dutch missionaries had won the good will of the mountain people, though the government had heavily taxed and exploited the Chinese on the plains. The present success of Christian work among the mountain tribes may owe something to an oral tradition stemming from these early Dutch beginnings.

Koxinga increased the island's food supply, using his soldiers in agriculture. He created a thriving export trade in rice, sugar, salt, and similar products. Cultural life was stimulated by the Chinese scholars and officials attracted to the developing island. In 1683 the Manchus conquered Taiwan and in the next two hundred years there were several mass migrations from the Chinese mainland. Able administrators in the nineteenth century developed irrigation and flood control projects, which, with increased trade, gave Taiwan greater economic prosperity and a higher cultural level than China herself.

From 1895 until 1945, when they surrendered to Chiang Kai-shek, the Japanese controlled Taiwan, despite a hundred or more local uprisings. They introduced improvements, but the Taiwan economy was made to serve Japanese interests. Half of the rice and five-sevenths of the sugar were shipped to Japan. The best land slipped into Japanese hands; education increased, but Taiwan students were prevented from advancing beyond high school; foreign economic enterprises were forced out. Fifty years of control, however, made their imprint. Many islanders, who learned to think in Japanese, now look back with nostalgia to the prewar days. They say that the Japanese police and courts were severe, but just.

The population is now nearing 11 million. Most of that number are Taiwanese: that is, Chinese originally from the Fukien area who have lived for centuries on the island. There are also many Hakka ("guest families" or "visitors") who have been in Taiwan for generations. The Hakka are a hardy people from China's Northwest who were forced out by Tartars in the thirteenth century. They are now spread over South China, Taiwan, and Hong Kong. In or near the mountains of Taiwan are the aborigines. Since 1945, after the

Chinese revolution, almost 2 million mainland Chinese arrived on the small island and assumed control of the government.

One tragic event embittered relationships and still plagues the government and churches. In 1947 the first postwar Chinese governor of Taiwan, who had alienated Taiwan opinion with a carpetbagging administration and plunder of Japanese properties, was confronted with demands from Taiwan leaders after a serious incident. He accepted the demands, then rounded up and executed the leaders in a reign of terror. The Kuomintang replaced the governor with a better man, but the memory of the early period cannot be erased.

The Nationalist Chinese thought of Taiwan as a temporary haven and started in to rebuild their army for a great effort to regain the mainland. The Taiwanese did not want Communist domination, but neither did they favor an enormous military effort to regain the mainland. If care and understanding had been used from the first, the two groups might have drawn closer together and still may—but it has not been easy and there is heat beneath the surface. Thus the mood of the people varies. The tea is both bitter and sweet. Many of the Nationalists are living on a diet of dreams, longing for the day when they will return to their families, their landholdings, and their position in the old society. These dreams are as hopeless as the revival of the old Southern plantation life in America. Whatever happens, the former society in China can never be re-established as it was. On cloudy days the Nationalists realize this, and are restless, and feel an island claustrophobia.

The Taiwanese are in their own home. They have had guests move in, take the front bedroom, change the numbers on the door, receive the mail, order the meals, and criticize the housework. But the Taiwanese, too, have memories, memories of what they had hoped for during the war: liberation, opportunities for their sons, developing of their island by their own initiative, and provincial autonomy such as they had in the early eighteen nineties. More patience is needed than may be available, although it is a tribute to Chinese courtesy and endurance that serious trouble has not developed.

Education

Elementary education is free and compulsory in Taiwan, and 95 per cent of all children of school age are in school. One out of every eight goes on to high school and many enter college, there being twenty-one institutions of higher learning on the island. These latter institutions attract, in addition to the local students, over 4,500 overseas Chinese and a few foreign students. Twenty-eight research institutes offer study, and vocational schools train some seventy thousand students. Less than 10 per cent of the adult population are illiterate and special classes are reducing this figure.

The psychological outlook of young college people is problematic. Criticisms are expressed, particularly in National Taiwan University where there is a degree of freedom. Not all students respond well to the repeated study of Dr. Sun Yat-sen's "Three People's Principles," the political foundation of the Republic. Underpaid teachers may contribute to the general dissatisfaction. University professors receive the equivalent of twenty-five dollars a month, plus housing and a rice subsidy. There is strong pressure among students to secure scholarships to America. Few return to Taiwan except those who have studied English or agriculture, for it is difficult to find adequately paid employment.

Economic and Industrial Problems

Taiwan has a fair proportion of natural resources, and an enterprising population with skilled technicians and good training centers. It is 55 per cent forested, and has fifty factories producing paper and pulp products. Over half of the power used is hydroelectric and the supply is being increased.

Steel mills and factories turn out motors, meters, electric fans, bicycles, pumps, and implements needed to mechanize agriculture. Two 36,000-ton oil tankers have been completed, the largest ships ever built by Chinese firms. One company is producing heavy trucks and diesel buses as well as small automobiles.

Textile production more than meets the domestic demand. Several million dollars' worth of handicraft products are exported annually or sold to tourists. Other important national products are sugar, fertilizer, cement, salt, aluminum, caustic soda, rayon filament, fluorescent lights, and canned pineapple. The problems are: over-production without adequate foreign markets; lack of standardization of quality; and insufficient modern banking facilities.

Most private industries in Taiwan are family owned. Other people seldom invest in them, perhaps from lack of confidence or because quicker returns can be secured through short-term personal loans. Interest of 40 or 50 per cent a year is common, and the going rate is about 33.5 per cent.

Agricultural products are the mainstay of Taiwan's export trade. Total farm production increases every year, but it is nearing the peak. If the population increases, Taiwan will have to expand fishery, forestry, and industrial development, attract additional capital, and manufacture more products for which she has the raw materials. The government is making a genuine effort to meet the situation, with an accelerated economic program and legislation offering incentives. Despite this, there is too little inflow of private capital. The American Aid Fund, exclusive of military support, has accounted for 30 per cent of the fixed capital formation in Taiwan during recent years.

American Aid

United States government economic aid to Taiwan in 1958-59 amounted to 70 million dollars. The aid programs account for one-third of the imports and 5 to 10 per cent of the gross national product. Most of the cotton, wheat, and edible oils used by the people are supplied in this way. In addition, the Development Loan Fund has made U.S. funds available for industrial and commercial projects. Agricultural commodities agreements have been signed, permitting the Chinese to secure surplus farm products, the purchase money to be used for educational exchange programs, economic development, mutual defense purposes, scientific cooperation, and agricultural trade. The adult population is aware of this aid and considers it the main factor in the raising of Taiwan's living standards.

Land Reform

The land reform program has been more successful than elsewhere in Asia, possibly because the legislature was controlled by mainlanders who were not, in Taiwan, the landlords. It was done in three stages: first, a reduction of rent from a 50/50 to a 75/25 basis; second, the selling of public land (formerly Japanese) to farmers; third, the enforced sale of private land down to a maximum holding of 7½ acres of rice land per person. The sale of public land reduced the

price of the landlords' land before the enforced sale. Landlords were paid in rice bonds and shares in government
enterprises. A problem was the unevenness of the compensation, since not all of the enterprises did well. There is un-
doubtedly resentment among the wealthier farmers.

An important by-product of the Land to the Tiller program
was the breaking up of the clan system representing the only
political power on the island outside of the Nationalist
party. Another disadvantage was the disappearance in rural
churches of wealthy laymen who could make generous contributions. The churches must now secure more small gifts,
which is healthy, but it increases the desire for outside aid.

The Standard of Living

The central government states that the people are better
off than they were under the Japanese, several American
experts agree with qualifications, but the Taiwanese complain
that they are worse off.

At the end of the war the island was desperate and production was low. The improvement since then has been
remarkable. Those who arrived after 1949 are therefore
correct in saying that they have seen substantial improvement. Older Taiwanese families claim, however, that prewar
living standards have not been surpassed. They have more
goods, more conveniences, but less security, less opportunity, less real wealth. There is almost no middle class now.
These critics say that, in spite of the 4½ per cent increase
in the national income, if allowance is made for the population growth, inflation, and other factors, there may even
have been a slight decline in the per capita income. The
important point is that many Taiwanese think that they are
worse off.

There is wealth on the island. The richest are a handful of mainlanders, but there is a larger group of wealthy Taiwanese. Yet, medical social workers in one city report that the average city dweller is getting poorer. The white-collar group is suffering. Fishermen are in need of relief the year around.

Mainlanders interested in rural reconstruction insist that the farmers' lot has improved; per capita rice production has increased, planting is more diversified, new houses are common, and the country people are better clothed. These observers believe the farmers support the government.

Commercialization of farm business has been intensified. It is easier for rural youth to earn money today, and they are less careful in spending it. Buses are serving the accessible villages. There is increasing rural electrification and use of power pumps for irrigation. Families own bicycles, modern furniture, sewing machines, and enjoy luxuries, movies, and listening to music. Rural sanitation and public health is better. Agricultural extension education, home economics programs for women, and 4-H club activities have improved.

There are complaints, however. With the change to smaller family units, older people feel neglected. One-third of the land given to the tillers has already gone back to the government since taxes could not be paid and the necessary fertilizer purchased. Farmers, in the past, felt secure with their land. Those who have had their holdings reduced do not feel as safe with shares in strange enterprises. Some leave farming entirely and set up shops, but often fail and are then without resources.

Two tendencies are dangerous: the rapid population increase, and the craze to spend money as it is earned, due to fear of inflation and uncertainty about the political future.

✳✳✳ 2 ✳✳✳

THE FOUR PEOPLES

The Taiwanese

Many of the Taiwanese have never seen China, their ancestors having been on the island since Cromwell's time. They speak the Amoy dialect, as different from spoken Mandarin (the national language) as Dutch is from English. They want to retain their language, but Mandarin is now compulsory in the schools. The older people read Japanese, but English has replaced it as the main foreign language.

The Taiwanese have a romanization for their dialect, which enables country people to learn to read quickly without using the difficult Chinese characters. They feel that mainlanders, by reinstating the characters, are forcing a cultural pattern that will make literacy unattainable for the masses. The issue is a serious one and has many overtones. It would be difficult for any people to change their language habits three times in seventy years. The Nationalists argue that romanization would cut off thousands of years of cultural history, and that Taiwan should be proud to come fully into the main stream of Chinese life. They believe that as the children learn Mandarin attitudes will change.

The older Taiwanese churches want the romanization retained so that they can have Bible-reading congregations and not illiterate ones. They feel that religious liberty is involved, the right of a church to determine how the Bible and hymn books shall be printed. In 1958, when the government ordered the churches to give up the use of romanized Bibles, a protest was filed. The government granted a delay of three years in enforcement. Some believe that the controversy is over, that the government will not force the issue. Others, in the government, believe that the church is using excuses to block the established language policy. They claim that it is not a religious problem but only stubborn provincialism among the older people.

The army is now half Taiwanese, though the higher posts are filled with mainlanders. There is no discrimination in education, and Taiwanese participation in government is increasing.

Although opportunities in public service are open to young Taiwanese, they are handicapped. A serious attempt has been made to find qualified Taiwanese for the diplomatic service, but few can compete with mainland applicants. The Taiwanese orientation has been Japanese, not international and Chinese. Higher education and many of the professions were not open to their parents. Few families owned libraries, traveled, and were competent in foreign languages and knowledge of Chinese history and etiquette.

Social problems—farm youth shifting to factories, unemployed ex-service men, the weakening of traditional morals, and resentment—have increased serious crime. The Taiwanese, paradoxically, blame it on too much democracy and freedom as compared with the stricter controls of the Japanese. The Nationalists believe that further education and citizenship training will increase voluntary observance of the law.

Many Taiwanese grievances are due to rapid changes in the family system and other established customs, and not to the evil intent of the government. However, because of the 1947 conflict and present differences, even changes in the weather are blamed on the Nationalists. The road ahead will be rocky. The thoughtful, reconciling forces on both sides need strengthening.

The Hakka Community

There are nearly 2 million Hakka, locally called "Cantonese," in Taiwan. They settled on the slopes between the Taiwanese on the good rice land and the tribes living in the mountains. Hakka are mostly agricultural, with a few engaged in fishing, and they are poorer than the Taiwanese. They are a conservative, strongly knit, disciplined group with their own patois and distinctive clothing (like the conservative Mennonites of Pennsylvania or the Russian immigrant groups in Canada). They are proud of their language and customs. They are considered native to the island now and could serve as a bridge, for they understand the mainlanders' difficulties, yet they are accepted by the Taiwanese.

The Hakka are industrious, particularly the women, who do harder outside work than the men. They plant tea, gather fuel for charcoal-making, grow sweet potatoes, and divert mountain streams into small, terraced rice fields. They have been neglected and have the psychology of an oppressed people, being seclusive, driving hard bargains, holding on to their money, and considered by others materialistic. A few are wealthy.

This community is the hardest one in Taiwan to evangelize, unlike the three hundred thousand Hakka in Hong Kong who have several strong churches. They are religious, adhering to a special form of Buddhism mixed with ancestor worship, Taoist elements, and animism.

In the past no Christian churches gave serious attention to the problem of language and custom involved in Hakka work. Now, the Canadian and Southern Presbyterians, the

Overseas Missionary Fellowship (formerly China Inland Mission) and others, have made a good beginning.
Church World Service has Hakka representatives on its executive committees. A Catholic priest has completed a Hakka
dictionary, and Protestants are working on Hakka romanization. Many Hakka can use the Amoy dialect but are not at
home in the romanization used by the Taiwanese churches.
Hakka youth have entered the ministry but usually serve
Taiwanese churches where the salary and schools for their
children are better.

The Mainlanders

The less than 2 million mainlanders in Taiwan are the
most powerful group politically and the ablest, since weaker
elements were left behind. They are intensely anti-
Communist, patriotic, sensitive to criticism, convinced that
they represent the only legal government of China, and determined to regain control of the mainland. They feel frustration at being restricted to the island, a claustrophobia such
as Napoleon must have felt on Elba. There is need for a
scapegoat, a need to maintain tension and a war psychology, a desire to strike out and assert again the will to power.
This is passing, but not gone. Mainlanders now talk in public
places about outlasting the Communist experiment, waiting
until internal dissension divides the mainland and it is possible to return without undue bloodshed. A few mainlanders
are settling for a permanent life on the island, with the hope
that the island's status can be stabilized. In this group and in
the army there is some intermarriage with Taiwanese, since
there are too few mainland girls.

A skeletal government representing the whole of China, as
well as Mongolian, Tibetan, and frontier tribal interests, has

been maintained by the Nationalists since 1948, also a large foreign affairs establishment and a standing army. To Taiwan Province, which is the only province paying taxes now, the highly developed structure of the central government seems to be unnecessary, undemocratic, top-heavy, and costly. Is it essential to a readiness for return to the mainland? The Nationalists insist that it is, and justify using Chinese personnel who know the mainland, the national language, and the ways of a Chinese government—which the Taiwanese do not.

Although the government of the Republic of China is now committed to a waiting policy, it actively broadcasts appeals to the other side of the Curtain. These broadcasts emphasize three points: that the communes are destroying the family; that, in economics, the Communists are failing and are inhumane when they export food while there are severe shortages; that political freedom exists outside, but despotism, of a sort that has never in China's history long survived, exists inside.

Corruption in Taiwan is mainly at the local and municipal level. The government at the top has seriously tried to root out corrupt practices. Taiwan's difficult political problems are not due to greedy officials feathering their own nests. There is some tax-dodging and minor dishonesties due to low pay. Other areas of corruption are found in business, industry, and the local judicial system. Industry is new and working out its own standards. Often owners, after making a profit, lend it out personally instead of putting it into improvements, reserve, or dividends. This second profit, to avoid taxation, may not appear on the books, but the company may be caught without cash and go bankrupt.

The Chinese police are less feared than were the Japanese,

and the courts, for political reasons, lean over backwards to assure that decisions will be popular. Japanese justice was inexorable. Now, the question is often asked, "Whom do you know?" There is some holding of people in jail without charge and, upon inquiry, the presentation of a red package (a gift) is suggested. These complaints point more to corruption in the Taiwanese community than in the central government. One charge, however, can be laid against the Nationalists: they claim credit for maintaining a high living standard in Taiwan, yet request, through international aid, more living commodities than does India with its much larger area and population. The aid should not be reduced, only the claims.

The Mountain Tribes

The earliest group on the island, two hundred thousand aborigines, are in seven major tribes, plus a few linguistic subdivisions. They resemble mountain tribes in the Philippines. Head-hunting was common, but Christian influence reached them before the war, despite strong Japanese opposition. During the war, tribal Christians were persecuted by the Japanese on the grounds that they worshipped an American god, despite tribal insistence that God had no nationality. After the war, there was a mass movement into the church. Now head-counting has displaced head-hunting as Protestants and Catholics vie for the allegiance of the new Christians.

The relations are good between the Nationalist government and the aborigines, who are permitted to come down from the mountains to the plains and settle on tax-free land between the east coast highway and the mountains.

The tribes are economically underprivileged, but the government is supplying them funds for building materials and house construction. Not all is well with them, however. Some fall into the hands of moneylenders, who charge high interest rates. The smaller tribes are losing their languages; their clothing is increasingly American-donated; they no longer weave their own distinctive cloth, though they do some basketry; their old culture is disappearing. Mountain women are coming out of the area and marrying Taiwanese or soldiers. The government encourages this for the sake of the unmarried soldiers, but the men in the mountains object. The women justify it on the ground that tribesmen turn into drunkards. Alcoholism is one of their typical problems.

The original tribal religions were animistic and superstitious. The growth of Christian churches has been so rapid since the war that the old views may have been covered over rather than consciously exchanged for sounder ones. The urgent need now is for persistent teaching and nurture. A Wycliffe translator is working to get the whole Bible into one of the languages. An English Presbyterian is reducing another one to writing and has helped to bring out a primer and a revised hymnbook. The Canadian Presbyterians have supplied a missionary for tribal language work, and there are others. All but two of the tribes will soon have the Scriptures in their own languages and provision of Christian literature is an urgent need.

Catholic work is expanding rapidly and has a strong children's program. The priests live with the tribes, whereas many of the Protestant workers itinerate.

Some Protestant churches are large. One has a thousand members and a choir of a hundred voices. In many churches they pay their own pastor. Their music is good and is being used in hymn books. These people love to dance and the church is making use of this in Christian programs. One folk dance is set to "Nearer My God to Thee." Taiwanese claim that the tribal churches are too emotional and the members so actively Christian that their farm work suffers, but they admit that the faith has helped them correct their addiction to heavy drinking.

There are 360 Presbyterian tribal churches with 60,000 believers, served by 31 ordained tribal ministers and 100 Bible School graduates, and also Holiness, True Jesus, Free Methodist, Baptist, Seventh-day Adventist, and Jehovah's Witness congregations. Mennonite medical teams have done a wonderful work in the treatment of leprosy and tuberculosis in the mountains. World Vision, Inc., and the Dicksons of the Canadian Presbyterians also have clinics, sanatoria, and relief and self-help projects. A Mount Morrison Theological and Agricultural Institute near Hualien and a Bible School at Hsinchu train tribal Christian workers.

Such are the four peoples who live together, for better, for worse, on "Formosa, the beautiful." Should the church speak from God's Word directly to the issues they face; reserve judgment but actively seek reconciliation; or preach the eternal Word and leave temporal issues to be decided by the U.N., Peking, America, or political struggle on the island?

✳✳✳ 3 ✳✳✳

THE RELIGIOUS SITUATION

In Taiwan all religions are showing new life as they are stimulated by the surprising growth of the Christian churches, or fostered as spiritual centers of national loyalty and of unity with other Asian peoples.

Buddhism

In recent years the number of Buddhist monks and nuns has risen to 830. New temples are being built and old ones redecorated, and Buddhist magazines and books are beginning to appear. Most country people are partially Buddhist, only taking part in occasional temple festivities. The Buddhists have allied themselves with the government and have helped to maintain stability and administer emergency relief. When war-time Japanese restrictions on popular temple festivals were removed, commercialized practices were introduced and feasts of tremendous size were held. Millions of dollars were spent. Older country people borrow money rather than lose face by not contributing to the temple feasts. Youth enjoy the feasts but feel the religious observances are old-fashioned. Children of Buddhist parents are taught little about religion.

Buddhists are attempting to enlist intellectuals in resisting the materialism that comes with industrialization and westernization. It is recognized that reliance on the self or the state has not been enough and a number of older government and military men have turned to Buddhism, but there is little support in the universities.

Confucianism

A Confucian revival has been sponsored by the government, and several Confucian magazines have been subsidized. Confucian animal sacrifices were tried for awhile but given up. Many mainlanders are agnostic, if they are not Christian, and the Taiwanese show no interest in the religious aspects of Confucianism. In 1960 the Society for the Study of Confucius and Mencius was organized. An earlier Confucian manifesto published by four scholars in Taiwan and Hong Kong combined neo-Confucianism with Hegelianism and Existentialism. They claimed that Confucianism was a down-to-earth, practical, humanistic religion, not dependent on worship, ritual, or sacrifice. They praised Christianity as one of the highest of men's faiths, but hard to understand and even more difficult to live since it demanded perfection. Confucianism alone could save the world, since it dealt clearly with family, social, and political relationships—things the common people could understand and practice.

The manifesto recognized both a religious need and a need for cultural cohesion. It appealed to intellectuals to return to something truly Chinese. It meant less to the Taiwanese with a Japanese cultural background. The writers suggested that Christianity undermined Chinese culture. They emphasized the Confucian faith in the goodness of man and the contribution it could make to a future world order.

The Nationalist party promotes Confucianism in the middle schools to combat liberalism, requiring the reading of the *Four Books* and the *Five Classics*.

The church in a Chinese setting must always interpret the Christian message with an understanding of its tension with this background of Confucian thought.

Other Non-Christian Religions

Taiwan's forty thousand Muslims have an imposing mosque in Taipei with more than religious value. King Hussein of Jordan worshipped there, as well as visiting Muslims from Indonesia, Malaya, and elsewhere. A five-man mission was sent to Mecca in 1959 and visited Pakistan to enlist support for freeing Chinese Muslims from Communist control and for helping refugees.

Taoism was introduced to Taiwan in the seventeenth century by Koxinga, who was later deified as a Taoist god. People burn incense to the spirits of his army. There are also temples to the God of Medicine and the God of War, to name two familiar deities. In the mornings and evenings or during funerals Buddhist or Taoist chanting can be heard in many rural homes.

On the Chinese mainland, Taoism is being persecuted more than any other religion for it has always ridiculed bureaucracy and harbors secret societies that turn political during national crises.

In Taiwan Taoism is mixed with the worship of Ma-Tsu, a female deity. The 1000th annniversary of her birth was celebrated recently in a costly two-day celebration. There is a local tradition that she preserved the first large migration of South Fukienese in their dangerous passage to the island.

The religious resurgence owes much to the general tension and desire for peace of mind. A high degree of mental disturbance is found among both Taiwanese and mainlanders. The people want assurance and a religion that will deeply satisfy them.

Christian Growth and Relationships

Dr. Hollington Tong once stated publicly that Christianity had become the dominant faith in Taiwan. The press and several officials denied this, for Christians number less than 6 per cent of the population. It is true, however, that no other faith has had more influence on the modern, educated segments of the population.

Protestant growth is 13 per cent per year, and Catholic growth 33 per cent, but statistics mean little unless accompanied by an equivalent growth in the quality of Christian living, the deepening of Christian faith, and the widening of Christian vision. At least two aspects of the church's life cause concern: relations within the Christian movement, and the scope of outreaching evangelism.

Relations between Protestants and Catholics could be improved. By 1959 over five hundred Protestant missionaries were working on the island with 1,200 national workers. Roman Catholics had over a thousand priests, sisters, and brothers. Ultra-Protestant groups are openly antagonistic to them. The priests often use better Chinese, discuss serious issues with students, and rely little on social parties and emotional meetings. In ten years their constituency grew from five thousand to more than two hundred thousand. Fu Jen, the former Catholic University of Peking, is being established in Taiwan with grants from the Pope and Cardinal Cushing, and a personal gift from President Kennedy. University officials hope to enroll twelve thousand students by 1965. A beautiful Catholic center has been built across the road from the Protestant Tung Hai University. Wise statesmanship is needed to prevent the situation from deteriorating into one of competition and ill-feeling.

A bewildering variety of Protestant denominations and sects have been in Taiwan since the war. Most had had work in China, but the multiplicity is more noticeable on an island. The Chinese army was at first open to Christian work, but sects took such advantage of the opportunity that the door was closed to all but one missionary. Proselytizing exists and comity is disregarded, yet zeal and love are also found, and God's work progresses despite the sad divisions of men.

Recently there has been an attempt from outside Taiwan to create discord among the Protestant groups. Permanent prejudices may develop as Christians call other church bodies such names as "modernist," "Communist," "obscurantist," "fundamentalist." An atmosphere of suspicion harms not only the church but the nation faced as it is with political enemies. Taiwan's very life, like Korea's, depends upon unity.

An equally serious danger is that suspicion of the World Council of Churches and the National Council of Churches in the United States may isolate the Christians of Taiwan from aspects of world Christian fellowship, including healthy Christian dialogue across political boundaries. The English Presbyterians, the Lutherans, and several other churches in Taiwan are keen about the World Council. Local congregations, however, are often reluctant even to share fully in the island-wide assemblies of their own church, let alone in the life of a World Council. At present, there is no National Christian Council in Taiwan. One missionary suggests that ecumenicity be redefined to include groups now outside the World Council.

The Taiwan Missionary Fellowship (350 mission representatives of larger denominations) brings some concert of action. It has no alignment with international organizations. There is also a Taiwan Evangelical Fellowship related to the World Evangelical Fellowship.

There have been mergers of related churches; the Taiwan Lutheran Church is aided by a mission that combines eight Lutheran boards from four countries; the Presbyterian Church of Formosa is related to five church bodies in three other countries. In the strong Tainan Theological College there is a ten-year-old example of Methodist, Episcopal, and Presbyterian co-operation. The German Marburger Mission, with devoted sisters who put all their personal resources into their work, co-operates with existing churches, as do members of

the Overseas Missionary Fellowship (C.I.M.) and the Free
Methodists.

Another co-operative event that contributed to main-
lander-Taiwanese understanding was the Consultative Conference on Protestant Church Work held by Presbyterian,
Episcopal, Methodist, and Lutheran representatives in 1960
and again in 1961.

Evangelism

Protestants are using many forms of evangelism: professional evangelists, visitation evangelism—especially by Bible
women—and meetings led by elders and church officers.
Members of large congregations are encouraged to start
chapels that the mother congregation helps until the new
churches get on their feet. Lay evangelists with partial high
school and Bible School training are preaching in small
chapels. In 1960 there were 233 ordained pastors for 1,478
organized Protestant congregations, also 533 evangelists, 80
catechists, and 133 Bible women.

One problem is inherited from the Japanese period. Authorities preferred to have churches build on inconspicuous
back streets, and have citizens register their religious affilia-
tions and stay in them. Police warned pastors to work solely
within their own constituencies. This encouraged the thought
that a particular church belonged to a group of congenial
families and existed to serve them only. Churches grew as the
families grew, but the missionary concern to reach strangers
and influence the community outside the church was little
emphasized.

One difficult problem in evangelism is fourth generation
Christians who take the faith for granted. Another is the
slackening of growth due to political frustration, hidden

bitterness in Taiwanese-mainlander relations, or unconfessed sins in relief goods distribution.

Christian Literature and Broadcasting

The production and distribution of Christian literature cuts across denominational lines. The earliest mission press on the island, the English Presbyterian in Tainan, supplies the needs of the many who read the romanized Taiwanese. The Christian Witness Press, the Baptist Press, and the Lutheran Literature Society maintain branches in Taiwan and there are many Christian book rooms. The China Sunday School Association is printing Uniform Lessons, and special materials for the tribal Sunday schools. In 1960 they doubled their distribution. A Christian Literature Association holds annual conferences. The Hong Kong Bible House, with an office in Taiwan and eight colporteurs, has increased its sales by one hundred thousand books each year since 1957. The Hong Kong Council on Christian Literature for Overseas Chinese also sends some literature to Taiwan. The Pocket Testament League, too, is active.

Christian broadcasting has grown remarkably since 1951. Twenty-one mission and broadcast organizations produce thirty-six programs that, with releases carried by commercial and government transmitters, fill 152 hours of radio time each week. The programs are broadcast in Taiwanese, Mandarin, Hakka, and English. A Taiwan Audio-Visual Education Association supplies films, slides, and related materials, and finds a warm welcome among rural people particularly.

Christian Education

The churches sponsor kindergartens, middle schools, colleges, universities, sixteen theological seminaries, and a number of Bible schools. The colleges and universities are: Tunghai University, supported by the United Board for Christian Higher Education in Asia; the Soochow University College of Law, affiliated with The Methodist Church, and offering work in six departments; and the Chungyuan Institute of Technology, an independent school founded by the Rev. James R. Graham.

Tunghai University has already achieved a wide reputation in Asia. It seeks to be loyally Christian and, also, to steep its students in China's cultural heritage. It is the only university in Taiwan to require every student to take two full years of Chinese. All of its students participate in a student-labor program. One-half of the staff at Tunghai are Christian and 20 per cent of the student body. No university in Taiwan selects its own students. All are assigned by the ministry of education after competitive examinations.

Soochow University has over a thousand students, a strong Christian Board of Managers, and on its law faculty ten judges from the supreme court of the Republic of China, including the President of the Court. Some Christians urge that Soochow University and Tunghai be related.

In the government schools no religious education is carried on, but missionaries may teach and may invite students to their homes. Some Protestant churches provide hostels next to government universities. Many students are agnostic. Immediately after the war, Venture for Victory, Orient Crusades, and other movements attracted large student audiences, but follow-up was inadequate. The students are friendly and courteous, but the level of communication is superficial until deep trust, fluency in Chinese, and common interests are developed. More trained student workers are needed. The Evangelical Alliance Mission (T.E.A.M.), Baptists, Lutherans, Presbyterians, Methodists, and others now have student centers. The Student Christian Movement works largely among Taiwanese students, and Intervarsity Fellowship works with mainlanders.

Young people compete intensely for places at all levels of education. The schedules are tight and students are over-loaded with assignments. Sunday schools are smaller because children study on Sunday in order not to lose their chance for advancement. The university load of required hours is abnormally heavy and makes for less creative work.

Bible schools in Taiwan concentrate on lay training, and the opening of neglected areas. They graduate a great many, but so far there has been no surplus of Christian workers.

Medical Work

After the Japanese left, public health deteriorated rapidly because of bubonic plague, malaria, and other diseases. Now, malaria has been reduced from a million cases a year to five hundred, and no cases are reported of cholera, typhus, smallpox, or scarlet fever. However, tuberculosis, leprosy, asthma and respiratory troubles, trachoma, and venereal diseases are serious. About half of the two thousand lepers are treated in Christian clinics. One expert thinks it may take twenty-five years to eliminate the incidence of leprosy. Christians are teaching cured lepers music, knitting, and other means of self-support.

A painful "blackfoot" disease attacks salt workers and fishermen in coastal villages. The World Health Organization is studying it. Meanwhile, amputation is used. One theological student, horrified at the conditions, appealed to a nearby Christian hospital and was offered two beds. He telephoned Mrs. Lillian Dickson of Taipei (who carries on a surprising variety of independent projects under the name Mustard Seed, Inc., with help from Bob Pierce of World Vision, Inc.). Mrs. Dickson immediately went by jeep to the village, offered twelve beds in one of her hospitals, transported the patients by taxi and jeep, then established a thirty-bed hospital in the coastal village, providing both a nurse and a physician. She combines direct evangelism with all her projects.

The Presbyterians have several hospitals, and the Lutherans, Mennonites, Catholics, Seventh-day Adventists, and other church groups are active in the medical field, some with mobile clinics. A dental clinic is run by a much-loved German Lutheran sister, who trains tribal dentists. Her dental students usually become Christian.

Christian Social Work and Church Relief

The church is beginning to train pastors and laymen for new responsibilities in this period of rapid social change. One institution now offers courses in social work, but the main emphasis is on sociology. Most welfare projects have to be run by people without specialized social work training.

Work in industrial evangelism has been started by George Todd in Tainan and Kaohsiung with wide Protestant cooperation. A Christian Workers' Center is to include a chapel, workers' education program, day-care for children of working mothers, vocational counseling and placement, family counseling, and a dormitory and youth center. In the Tainan and Taipei Theological Seminaries courses are now offered on such subjects as "Church and Industry," and "Church and Juvenile Delinquency." Short conferences for Christian businessmen are held, and Bible study has been started in factory groups and literature made available. A fellowship of young ministers near factory areas has been organized. Theological students may join summer seminars in industry.

Shipments of food, clothing, and medicines handled by church welfare agencies in 1958-59 were in excess of three million dollars. The two Protestant agencies, Church World Service and Lutheran World Relief, have combined operations and import 50 per cent of the surplus food, the other half going to Catholic relief services.

The aid is well distributed now. Only those who do not pay taxes receive it. The Chinese government makes out the list. One month the Catholics take charge, the next month the Protestants. Since both distributions go to the same people, the charge that the churches use the food to increase their own membership is avoided. Milk powder is processed but not given directly. Flour is often made into noodles.

The Protestants have over six hundred distributors in local churches. They give the relief goods first to those listed but if there is any left over, they are permitted to give 20 per cent to their own members. The time it takes to distribute relief intelligently is greater than many of the churches can afford, so there is always a temptation to do it the easy way. Rules and constant supervision are necessary.

Is continued aid making people dependent, or enabling them to work with more energy and hope? Some Christians feel it is undermining the sense of stewardship in the churches and causing mutual suspicion. Church World Service and Lutheran World Relief advocate a shift to projects producing self-support, but they realize that food distribution should not be stopped entirely or abruptly. They already have development projects (sewing centers, handicraft work, agricultural programs, and student manual labor), medical assistance, and immmigration and adoption help.

An "Evangelical Academy" movement for lay discussion of practical issues is needed in Taiwan. There is a postwar tendency to focus the gospel upon the personal areas of life in which men are most conscious of estrangement from God, leaving out the other areas of intellect and social conscience in which men have equally fallen short. Many missionaries and pastors fear that C.W.S. and other welfare programs in the churches introduce secular interests, though they want aid increased rather than stopped. They have been trained to think of spiritual need in individuals rather than of whole persons in communities. The combination of a purely spiritual message and a material gift of surplus products is not a full and integrated evangelism. May God help us to sense human need at all levels of that need, and understand the Word of God in its full relevance.

✳✳✳ 4 ✳✳✳

HOPE VERSUS LIMITATIONS

If you see the beauty and the resources of Taiwan, you are impressed. If you talk with the people, you are moved by their energy and faith. If you examine the problems, you are disturbed and cautious in any optimism.

Divisions

The division between the Taiwanese majority and the Nationalists continues, and it is serious. It has an economic basis. In the past the four hundred thousand Japanese were no competitive danger to the Taiwanese pedicab drivers, street stall operators, and other low income workers. Now mainlanders compete for jobs the Japanese would not accept. Higher up the scale in private business, the Taiwanese have the money. Feeling between one group holding money and another political power is to be expected. Taiwanese businessmen resent the taxes they have to pay to support an artificially large government and army. The mainlanders complain that they are considered alien and that the Taiwanese do not share the land or other economic opportunities with them. Some mainlanders treat the Taiwanese as though they had all been collaborators and therefore past or potential enemies.

The feeling is worse in the south around Tainan, the traditional capital, and Kohsiung and Pingtung. In the old crystallized society there, the landowning class is more important. The government's land reforms hurt them. On the east coast and southeastern tip, where the struggle for a living is harder, relations between the two groups are much better.

In any board meeting the voting is likely to be mainlander versus Taiwanese no matter what the issues are. The Taiwanese say this will last as long as political power is retained by a minority; that their children soon learn in society that the basic interests of the two groups are different. They realize that the mainlanders cannot share the power, for if they did they would be put out of power.

The Taiwanese do not have the same emotional feeling about communism that the mainlanders do. They have not seen it. An unexperienced totalitarian oppression is not as real as the present thwarting of Taiwanese wishes. Censorship of books and removal of sections of encyclopedias foster a feeling of dictatorship, even though it is a mild one. They also feel no passion to share in the struggles of six hundred million people whose standard of living is lower than their own. They are probably like the non-Zionist Jews who feel genuinely Hebrew but not Israeli in a nationalist sense. The Taiwanese are Chinese but not at home in their racial culture. They complain, for example, that the university examinations, which stress Chinese literature and history, are weighted against them.

It would be to the interest of the Communists to exploit the divisions, but there is little evidence of open Communist activity on the island. A group of Taiwanese in Japan are working for an independent Taiwan but they have only a few sentimental adherents on the island, receive little attention, and apparently have no effective organization. The Taiwanese as a whole seem to feel that they cannot bodily remove the mainlanders and that as long as economic conditions remain relatively satisfactory, there is no compulsion to risk their lives.

The government is making some progress among the younger people. In Tunghai University, students are put in dormitories alphabetically, thus mixing Taiwanese and mainlanders. Later, when they may choose their associates, they usually stay together. The younger generation are forgetting the 1947 incident and can now speak Mandarin. But it is hard to tell how happy these young people are, or what they are thinking, as Taiwanese do not speak frankly. It could affect their future. They are not in a rebellious mood but suffer from lassitude. Floating along, hoping for bureaucratic jobs, they are often swirled into a flood of youth parades and rallies in addition to their heavy academic assignments.

Some observers note a softening of the temper of the debate, a decrease in arbitrary arrests and imprisonments without trial, and greater patience among the Taiwanese. This improvement is said to be due to social services aiding both groups; complete opening of higher education; increasing intermarriage—though it is not uncommon for parents to refuse to let their daughters marry mainlanders; and occasional employment of mainlanders in Taiwan business houses.

In church gatherings the Taiwanese will speak freely in the presence of the Hakka but not of the mainlanders. Few mainlanders are learning Taiwanese. This is disturbing to the older Christians, who think of Taiwan as the cultural capital of the Amoy-speaking churches in the Philippines, Malaya, and southeast Asia. The church could help tremendously by inducing both groups to clarify the issues and face them frankly together. It is spiritually unhealthy for Christians year after year to commemorate Christ's supreme act of reconciling love while harboring unresolved resentments and carefully sheltered suspicions. The synagogues and the temple in Christ's day were unhealthy in the same way and did not like his cleansing ways, or understand why he wept over their condition and prospect.

A few churches in Taipei, Tainan, and the Hualien area, have begun to minister to both groups in the two languages.

Population and Land Hunger

The rapidly growing population in Taiwan can be supported on the available land now with care and planning; after 1970, with difficulty; but not after 1980, when the population will have reached twenty million. That figure is given as the maximum the island can support. The eleven largest cities have doubled in population in the last ten years, Taipei has tripled, and Kaohsiung has quadrupled. Basic food production has not increased as rapidly. The death rate has been decreasing but not the birth rate. Already the density of population per square mile of cultivated land is higher than the average figure for China as a whole. In 1957, if the cultivated land had been divided equally among the people, no one would have received a third of an acre. Country people are concerned because each year houses, roads, factories, and military bases encroach upon the cultivatable land.

The government is letting a few older, prosperous farmers emigrate to Latin America, after which younger people may move in and subdivide the land. Chinese leaving the island, including those going for temporary visits, must obtain exit permits, but the government grants only about four thousand a year. People are urged to migrate to the east coast but not many do, for the soil is poor. The cross-island highway, opened in 1960, will make some resettlement possible, but it will mean more to businessmen opening inns and restaurants than to farmers seeking land. However, a start has been made to grow fruit, vegetables, and seeds in the newly opened mountainous area, and plans for grazing are being studied. There is also a program for recovery of 123,550 acres of tidelands on the west coast.

A greater degree of industrialization would raise income and lower the birth rate, but it depends upon increased American investment loans, or the attraction of private capital.

A China Family Planning Association, aided by the Joint Commission on Rural Reconstruction, and social work agencies, has been carrying on a limited birth control program, but in rural areas young couples are discouraged by the lack of information and the cost. There is also a population study society. Rural marriages take place now five or six years later than formerly, since more young people are studying beyond high school or serving in the army, and parents no longer insist on grandchildren as early as before.

Return to the Mainland

The current doctrine on "return to the mainland" is that it must be in the context of a mainland revolution. Political means are suggested in place of all-out military ones. It is believed that a good society in Taiwan will be a factor in persuading the mainland millions that the Nationalist government should be invited back. In the meantime government and party in Taiwan do what they can to influence the situation across the straits. The crucial question is, can Taiwan wait indefinitely, yet maintain a good standard of living and a satisfactory political life? Under normal circumstances it might, but the circumstances are not normal. Can hope be fed year after year on postponement, and internal problems await the end of a permanent military crisis? Is there a moral equivalent for war that can sustain unity, morale, and prolonged social effort? These problems plague the mainland also.

Free Speech and Democracy

The party in power believes there is freedom of the press. The Taiwanese do not. Lei Chen's group published *Free China. Forum* and *China Today* express a Taiwanese point of view (the part that can be expressed), and the *China Post* is at times critical. However, the frank speaking and writing that exists is not about the central issues. The island is small and Communist threats from the mainland are loud and vociferous. The government is in a state of watchful tension. Criticism is easily interpreted as treason; a plea for natural rights as self-interest; a cry for justice as divisiveness or provincialism. The Kuomintang (Nationalist party) advocates one party rule because the country is at war. Competition and criticism of authorities are discourteous from a Confucian point of view. The Nationalists claim that all intelligent and able men are welcome in the ranks of the one party. The Taiwanese see flaws in this.

Would genuine alternative parties, free speech, and democratic procedures endanger the island's stability? They might, while the present undercurrent of bitterness is strong. During the Korean student riots that unseated Syngman Rhee, wall newspapers appeared near the universities in Taiwan urging the students to follow suit. Before President Eisenhower's visit, wall newspapers appeared again with slogans similar to those used by Japanese students: "We don't want you." In the presidential election in Taiwan, some of the posters urging that the Generalissimo be re-elected were defaced. These actions may have been entirely spontaneous and patriotic, but it is also possible that outside influences were seeking to exploit the bitterness, using volatile students to build up a wider civil disturbance. In a situation full of risk the government will not take chances with "dangerous" freedoms. But continued restriction of freedom may be even more dangerous.

The elections are nominally free, but better qualified Taiwanese are not campaigning, and unofficial groups are not permitted to watch the elections. Many Taiwanese consider the local and provincial elections a façade and the candidates ambitious servants of the Kuomintang rather than of the people. The directives come from above. No elected officers can touch education or the police. Taiwanese have been elected as mayors of cities, but the situation does not attract men who want responsible government. The two smaller recognized parties, the Young China Party and the China Democratic Socialist Party, came to Taiwan with the Nationalists. They split into factions penetrated by the

Kuomintang, discredited by local people, and have no hope of implementing a program. Essentially they are political clubs. Each claims some Taiwanese members, but endorsement by either one is a handicap in an election.

President Chiang Kai-shek's prestige is still tremendous. He is thought to be above all the groups and cliques. Many who criticize the government prefer him to any of the other top officials. He has, however, never understood the political value of opposition in the practice of democracy.

There are ultraconservatives among the Nationalists who believe that the central government is already too democratic and weak. One professor published a booklet accusing the Nationalist government's Dr. Hu Shih of losing the mainland, an accusation as irresponsible as the one that claims General Marshall lost it.

American Policy

Western, especially American, interests in Taiwan are contradictory. Americans have an emotional and moral interest in supporting a former ally in a period of hardship, and a military and political interest in having Taiwan part of a co-operative system of defense against Communist expansion. However, we have an equal interest in representative government and an urgent need for evidence that a free democratic economy is a way to prosperity under Asian conditions. But genuine democracy would put in power a Taiwanese majority with no will to maintain a costly military structure, no experience in statesmanship, and no tested anti-Communist passion. Thus traditional American aims and ideals and immediate strategic needs contradict each other and the months go on swirling round and down the drain of the dilemma.

At present American military advisers in Taiwan seem to lead a charmed life. There are irritations, particularly when anything borders on arrogance. But the advantages of American aid are well known. The agricultural program reached the remote countryside with concrete benefits and, in the cities, the aid to industries has been noticeable. Americans have given the impression that they are fun-loving, generous, rough, naïve persons. This is partly due to the segregation of American staff, which creates its own problems. The American officers have separate clubs and air-conditioned offices and live apart from the Chinese. This equally prevents incidents and understanding. Dependence upon U.S. policy decisions adds to Chinese frustrations, and American wealth, habits, and influence upset Chinese cultural patterns. The church, with no nationality, can move in the quiet depths below such a frozen situation and interpret and reconcile at deeper levels.

What alternatives do the government and people of Taiwan face? They can embark on a desperate military venture, against the advice of the free world, and possibly lose everything. They can seek to maintan the present stalemate indefinitely, but run the risk of defeat in the United Nations and greater isolation, with America forced to decide how far she can proceed alone in support of a republic no longer recognized by other nations. They can accept a two-China concept while there is time to negotiate in the United Nations for mutual defense and adherence to a bloc that would guarantee Taiwan against absorption by Communist China. The question of the welfare of the Taiwanese people and the degree of democracy that can be realized on the island will remain unsettled, probably, until one of the above decisions is made. None of the alternatives are satisfactory, and any decision will be difficult—perhaps politically impossible to make. In this case, world events and distant judgments will shape free China's destiny. The men who face these issues and bear the responsibility for decision need understanding and prayer more than they need the easy criticism of observers.

HONG KONG

*** 1 ***

HISTORY, CULTURE, AND IMPORTANCE

Hong Kong is a place of contrasts—with its natural beauty and its artificial flowers, with its winding hill roads overlooking dark and crowded tenements, with its beehive busyness counterpointed by the incessant clatter of mahjong, with its delectable food and tempting shops and its hungry, homeless children, with its perennial tragedy and its spontaneous gaiety. But it is a rebuilding, ever-hopeful, unbelievable free port.

Hong Kong has been called "an illuminated cemetery" yet it overflows with life. It is full of haunting beauty—and of haunting memories for many whose relatives have been left behind on the other side of the Bamboo Curtain. The tourist who climbs among the hillside huts, or to the crowded city roof-tops, will also have haunting memories. Hong Kong is a place of hope for the future, and of anxiety for tomorrow. It is a heart-warming place, because the people are so industrious, so cheerful, so responsive; and a heart-breaking place because there aren't enough jobs, enough houses, enough schools, enough answers to the many pressing problems.

Physical Characteristics

The total land area of this British colony is 398 square miles, comprising Hong Kong island, Kowloon, and the New Territories. It has over 240 islands and one of the most perfect natural harbors in the world. The area is rugged and mountainous, only sixty-two square miles being usable.

Hong Kong has hot weather from May to November but a cool winter from January through March. The autumn is dry and pleasant. It is a windy place and gets the edges of typhoons in the summers, but it is seldom hit by the center of a serious one. Some eighty-five inches of rain fall between May and September. There are signs of old beaches four hundred feet above the present sea level and a shore line one hundred feet lower than the present one, suggesting a deep submergence in recent geological times, and a progressive uplift with marked changes since—as with the human situation.

Over three hundred species of birds frequent Hong Kong. A few porcupines, scaly anteaters, rhesus monkeys, and barking deer are around, though they are more reticent about public appearances, as the multitudes of human beings take over with their opposite tendencies. The main trees of the colony are pine, banyan, and camphor. At one time Hong Kong's prosperity rested upon camphor and other fragrant woods for coffins and carved chests. The flowers of Hong Kong range from clematis, wild violets, honeysuckle, begonias, wild iris, and lilies, to equatorial orchids, lotus, magnolias, poinsettias, and camellias.

Early Developments

From prehistoric times trading people from farther south have lived seasonally on the islands. Settlements of Chinese were continuous in the area from the thirteenth century on. The first regular shipping was Arab, bearing Indian, Persian, and Jewish traders, who formed a foreign community farther inland in Canton. In the sixteenth century the Portuguese stopped the Arab trade and secured Macao, forty miles from Hong Kong. Seasonal British trade with China began about 1700.

The trade in Canton grew and the British negotiated for a small island or port where they could reside permanently under their own laws. They were unsuccessful. The East India Company's China monopoly ceased in 1833. Among other things it had forced British traders to obey Chinese regulations. Thereafter, the number of traders, including Americans, increased and each acted on his own, although the Chinese insisted upon collective responsibility. The demand for the surrender of a foreign national after a Chinese had been killed helped to precipitate the Opium War.

The underlying economic cause of this strange little conflict was the desire of Europeans to secure Chinese silk, tea, lacquer, and other products, while they were unable to exchange equivalent amounts of European goods. Traders first used silver and then began to barter with opium from nearby India. This affected the silver standard in South China and increased addiction. The Chinese government demanded the surrender of all opium and the signing of bonds never to bring in any more. The Americans and others signed while the British surrendered the opium but refused to sign the bonds. Relations deteriorated, the British community moved to Macao, were refused protection, and finally anchored in the harbor of Hong Kong. Hostilities broke out. The British again demanded an island or normal trading rights. The Manchu negotiator offered Hong Kong.

In 1841 the rocky island was occupied and the cession was confirmed by treaty in 1842. Kowloon was added by treaty in 1860 and in 1898 the New Territories were leased by the British government for ninety-nine years.

Hong Kong was a free port for both trade and people, and rose and fell like a bellows manipulated by events in China. Soon after its foundation great waves of emigrants came through on their way to the Straits Settlements, Thailand, and Java, and, later, to the gold fields of California and Australia.

Education was first provided by missionaries, Catholic and Protestant, and was an outgrowth of a great missionary thrust, for Hong Kong was used by the church as a staging point for evangelization of the great continent against which it lay. Hospitals, too, were established by missionary effort. Because of natural calamities, and the ever increasing population, there has always been a strong local interest in social welfare.

European and Chinese commerce in Hong Kong developed independently, linked only by Chinese compradores who assisted the foreign merchants. But the demand for Western education increased, and with it a gradual adoption of Western business methods. St. Paul's College, for example, which was started by Anglicans primarily "for the training of . . . clergy and Christian teachers for the propagation of the Gospel in China," soon found that commercial openings for Chinese who spoke English were so lucrative that few of the graduates were devoting themselves to the missionary enterprise. By the end of the century, there were Chinese shipping lines, banks, department stores, insurance companies, theaters, factories, and other business enterprises too numerous to mention.

Contemporary Hong Kong

Hong Kong has dramatic contrasts of poverty and wealth and of Eastern and Western ways of life. Repulse Bay is like the Riviera. A mile or two away in Aberdeen the smoke of cooking and the murmur of conversation rise through a tight forest of swaying junk and sampan masts. Wanchai is the world of Susie Wong, while on the slopes of the peak above it are the beautiful homes and gardens of families of wealth and the diplomatic community. One would expect Hong Kong to develop violent resentments, but the city peacefully spoils the predictions of sociologists and prophets. Hong Kong is a many-leveled place and, perhaps, the moles, the fish, the butterflies, and the hawks do not see each other.

Hong Kong has the same significance in Asia as has Berlin in Europe. It is important as the main center of contact between Communist China and the non-Communist world. The dividing Curtain is not as rigid as the one separating the two Koreas. Between Hong Kong and China there is daily traffic of people and goods in both directions, under restrictions imposed by both sides. At present, the colony serves the interests of East and West sufficiently to be let alone. The area could not be defended long, but the cost of taking it and the consequent loss of its value as a free, neutral port outweigh any advantage that would be gained. Hong Kong, therefore, shows a surprising stability, both financially and politically. But its internal problems are many. Water is one of them. The huge population depends upon rain-catchment. There are periods every year when the water in the pipes is rationed—sometimes use is restricted to two hours out of every twenty-four. Daily, hundreds of children can be seen toiling up the hillside slopes with heavy buckets of water drawn from the public spigots. In 1956 the reservoirs held

4,647 million gallons. New reservoirs are being added, and water is also piped from a reservoir on the other side of the Curtain.

The population of Hong Kong is over 99 per cent Chinese. It is ruled by a British Governor, with an Executive Council, a Legislative Council (each containing several Chinese members), and thirty departments manned by a Civil Service under the direction of a Colonial Secretary. An Urban Council has a few places for elected members. A Reform Club and a Civic Club put forward candidates and act as parties. The electorate is small, but there is little insistent demand for political responsibility. The colony has nothing to exploit, is extremely conscious of local Chinese sentiment, and has had a series of wise governors. Many residents seem content to have found this neutral haven in a divided world.

Economic Conditions

Hong Kong is one of the few territories in the world that retain both free enterprise and free trade. Business men of any nation can start concerns in Hong Kong on equal terms with local enterprise, and they may freely remit profits or repatriate capital. There is a profit tax of 12½ per cent, and a low, graded personal income tax. Public debt seldom amounts to more than eight weeks' normal revenue.

In the stream of refugees after World War II there came many with capital and with business and technical experience. Additional capital flowed in from Chinese communities in southeast Asia. When Hong Kong's trade with China was reduced by American and U.N. embargoes and Communist restrictions, it was this Chinese initiative, skill, and capital, plus the abundance of good cheap labor, that saved the colony from economic collapse by effecting a rapid shift from trade to industry. By 1959 there were 5,023 registered factories and many smaller domestic industries, despite the absence of special benefits and the shortage of water, level land, fuel, and raw materials. Today the government is reclaiming land from the sea for industrial development. Twenty-two factories are already operating on the first completed site of the 452 acres scheduled for reclamation.

The colony builds or repairs over 450 ships a year. It is also the world's largest ship-*breaking* center, and uses a portion of this scrap to turn out six thousand tons a month of reinforcing bars from its own rolling mills. Hong Kong's major industry is textiles, and it has up-to-date spinning mills and looms that produce over 340 million square yards of cloth a year. Its tailoring is well-known. It exports a wide variety of other products ranging from cheap felt hats to plastic flowers.

The United States and Canada have been increasing their trade with Hong Kong. Together they represent the largest market for its products. Further income is received from the approximately two hundred thousand American tourists that pass through each year, spending several million dollars, and from the ten thousand American military personnel who visit the colony for rest and recreation every month.

The labor situation is complex. There are too many unions and they are all political. Those on the left, which support Peking policies, are in the Federation of Trade Unions with about sixty-five affiliated and twenty-five co-operating unions. Those on the right, which support Taiwan policies, are in the Trades Union Congress with seventy-two affiliated unions and fifty-three co-operating groups. Thousands of workers are unorganized and there is a big backlog of unemployed. These conditions tend to inhibit serious labor disputes. If one union walks out it cannot get the co-operation of unions of a different political persuasion. Hong Kong is thus a managerial paradise, if such a term can be used to describe a grim human situation. Under the circumstances, most unions prefer to waive, temporarily, questions of hours and wages, striving mainly for welfare benefits, education, and the political adherence of members.

Workers with steady employment work seven days a week, so are not churchgoers. A small committee on industrial evangelism is active, publishing a news sheet, holding conferences, and relating the churches of Hong Kong to this neglected field. Among the problems the workers face are low wages; long hours; organizational conflict (many prefer to stay out of political unions); insufficient welfare help; lack of nurseries for their children where both parents work; insecurity (day laborers without contracts may lose their places if they get sick); and a lack of a public opinion forum through which issues may be discussed. An informed church could be a great help to them. Many workers think of the church as serving people of leisure who don't have to work on Sunday and as helpful to Christians, but not interested in the welfare of non-Christians.

Housing

Next to the rapid development of industry, the most startling postwar feature of Hong Kong has been the building boom, which is related to the influx of refugees. Private building goes up at a cost of over 47 million dollars a year. In addition, the government has built housing for some 270,000 refugee "squatters" during the period, 1954-1960, and is adding new units at the rate of a hundred thousand a year. Middle income families have not been neglected either.

In four years the Hong Kong Housing Authority provided for 91,000 such earners, and co-operative societies and other non-profit agencies, using government funds, have built flats for over 106,000. Moreover, twenty thousand persons are being relocated annually from older, substandard buildings, and thousands of others have been housed in new little cottages erected by government and church agencies on marginal land. So far, the Hong Kong government has met the capital cost of its tremendous housing schemes without outside aid or public borrowing, for the colony believes in self-help and trade in preference to aid.

Despite such heroic efforts, the crowding is as bad as anywhere in the world. In some places population density is measured at four thousand persons per acre. There are still some six hundred thousand squatters living in hillside huts (fire has repeatedly ravished these areas, making tens of thousands homeless) and the Hong Kong government, which has housed in resettlement blocks more people than the entire population of Cincinnati, must keep on building to provide for them. In these blocks each 10 foot by 12 foot room houses a family of five adults (each child under ten is considered as one-half of an adult) and smaller families must double up. In most other housing, accommodations are shared, and only one family out of every thirteen has a living room that is not used for sleeping.

Hong Kong has been most generous in opening its doors to the human flood from mainland China and has been doing its utmost to provide housing, health facilities, schools, and employment. Of course, several million dollars a year in goods and money flow from the British Commonwealth nations and the United States in the form of government, private, and church aid for the refugees. The Scandinavian countries and West Germany have also made contributions. But the costs of aid are overwhelming and Hong Kong should not be expected to bear the major share of the total burden of this world problem.

Education

Hong Kong is important as now containing a cross section of the entire population of China, and as drawing an increasing number of students from the Chinese communities of southeast Asia. It has long been a commercial center, is now an industrial center, and is fast becoming a cultural center. Chinese merchants as far away as Indonesia are sending their children to Hong Kong for education in private schools. If Hong Kong became a strong Christian center, its influence would penetrate resident Chinese communities from Japan to Burma and south to Australia.

Hong Kong is not only a crossroads of peoples, but of ideas and of cultures. Four distinct ways of life influence youth in Hong Kong: militant Marxism, Confucianism, Western secular materialism, and the Christian way, which is distinctly different from all three, yet inclusive of some parts of each.

Private organizations, including churches, have opened over one thousand schools in the colony since 1946, the present rate being one new school every two weeks, while the government opens a new primary school every two months. By the end of 1961, 306,000 new places had been provided in primary schools, yet many schools still run two or three sessions. There are schools on flat roof-tops, in apartment houses, in labor union headquarters, in churches, wherever space can be found. The colony's Education Department is active in maintaining standards and does a magnificent job with the fast-moving belt of oncoming children, ten thousand new ones being born every month (though Hong Kong's most valuable product, there is overproduction).

Thousands of children are not in school. Many are helping their parents by making matchboxes, carrying babies on their backs, hauling water, and shining shoes. Other thousands, with both parents away at work, are growing up unsupervised. Children are everywhere; one steps on them, is pestered by them, thanks God for them, tries to forget them, and is haunted by them. They are the hope of the future, and, if more is not done, its potential curse. In a few years they may be hardened by street life till they cannot trust anyone, even Christ, having burned out all emotion in fruitless bids for love.

Throughout the world church, the children must be a continuing part of the concern for Hong Kong. There are two needs: the first is for emergency child-care programs, feeding programs, nurseries, boys' and girls' clubs, playgrounds, and centers for child beggars; the second is for long-range school planning. Christian schools are welcome in Hong Kong if they have high standards and a well trained staff. This requires time, money, and continuing responsibility, but the human rewards are great.

There are two parallel educational streams, with Chinese as the medium of instruction in one and English in the other. The University of Hong Kong is a private institution, largely supported by government grants, that uses English. Now accommodating 1,400 students, it is planning for a larger enrollment. The university is good, but expensive, and many Chinese find it difficult to qualify in English. In addition, a technical college teaches in English, and there are some seven post-secondary colleges teaching in Chinese.

The post-secondary colleges are a refugee contribution to the cultural life of the colony, and provide training for several thousand students. The University and the colleges together do not offer enough places for the students who clamor for higher education. Quite a few go to universities in Taiwan, or to mainland Chinese universities, or apply for places overseas. There are usually over 1,500 studying in the United Kingdom, several hundred in Canada, more in Australia, over a thousand in the U.S.A., and others in Japan, the Philippines, and other Asian countries. The welcome and influences they meet in these lands are factors in shaping the Hong Kong of the future.

Two of the post-secondary colleges are Christian. Chung Chi has the united support of many of the churches of Hong Kong and has received generous aid from the United Board for Christian Higher Education in Asia (New York), the Asian Christian Colleges Association (London), the Hong Kong government, foundations, and individuals. Its campus is in a beautiful valley between the city of Kowloon and the border. Forty per cent of the co-educational student body is Christian, and they carry on an active worship, witness, and voluntary service within the college community and in neighboring orphanages and villages. The college, with Tunghai University in Taiwan, continues the traditions of the thirteen former Christian colleges and universities of China. Nearly half of Chung Chi's five hundred students are refugees, and usually one student in every seven is from a Chinese community in Borneo, Sarawak, Singapore, Malaya, or elsewhere in southeast Asia. Many of the students are dependent upon scholarship, loans, or self-help work.

The Hong Kong Baptist College is building a new campus in Kowloon and strengthening its academic program with the help of Southern Baptists in the United States. New Asia College is a private institution related to the Yale-in-China overseas program, while the United College was formed from a union of five separate institutions. It is hoping to build a beautiful new campus on the island of Hong Kong.

There is now a movement to develop a federated Chinese University with degree-granting privileges, parallel to the University of Hong Kong. Toward this end Chung Chi, New Asia, and the United College have formed the Joint Colleges Council under a set of post-secondary college regulations drawn up by the government. Each college is to retain its autonomy and special characteristics. These institutions are attempting something of great significance: a new integration of Eastern and Western learning in an atmosphere of academic freedom and mutual respect.

✳✳✳ 2 ✳✳✳

THE MULTITUDES AND THEIR PROBLEMS

A visitor to Hong Kong remarked that she had never fully understood the meaning of Jesus' compassion on the "multitudes" until she was caught in the flow of people along its busy streets. Hong Kong was overcrowded before Pearl Harbor, but had shrunk to six hundred thousand by the end of the war. Between 1949 and 1951 population increased rapidly. Later, thinking that the movement in and out of China could be equalized, the Hong Kong government lifted its restrictions by agreement with Peking. Within four months limitations had to be enforced again, for eighty thousand more Chinese came out to stay in Hong Kong than returned to the mainland. The movement still continues, both by entry permit and illegally. Over a third of the population is under fifteen, only 5 per cent are sixty or over, and males outnumber the females up to middle age. Though Hong Kong's population increased from two to three million between 1951 and 1960, deaths decreased, since the public health services are good, the climate mild, and the average refugee quite young.

Welfare Activities

Welfare organizations in Hong Kong have shifted to rehabilitation projects from the early feeding, clothing, and relief programs, except for care for fire and typhoon victims, children, and the destitute. In addition to the excellent work of the Social Welfare Department of the government there are fifty-two voluntary agencies co-operating in the Hong Kong Council of Social Service, plus others not related to it. An employment program locates jobs for hundreds and a resettlement loan association assists those who want to start small businesses. Beggars are being removed from the streets through the use of cards introducing them to welfare agencies.

The Hong Kong Christian Welfare and Relief Council has been giving priority to self-help projects for families, to the college student work projects, and to the enlarging of facilities for tuberculosis patients. Sixty thousand beds are needed at once instead of the two thousand that are available. Tuberculosis spreads because of overcrowding and kills six times as many people as all other infectious diseases and ten times as many as in the United States. The Christian Council also helps rural and forestry resettlement projects, the rehabilitation of drug addicts, ecumenical work camps, and a vocational training program. A Boys' and Girls' Clubs Association enrolls twelve thousand children in 203 clubs and provides in-service training for leaders. The Christian Children's Fund and the Foster Parents' Plan, Inc. assist orphans and needy children. Lutheran World Service carries on a wide program of medical care, vocational training, self-help, and material relief. The Church of Christ in China, a union of several denominations formerly active on the mainland, supports a family welfare center, vocational training, children's work, case and group work, and medical and industrial welfare programs. Active welfare work is also carried on by the Anglicans, Methodists, Baptists, Mennonites, Y.M.C.A., Y.W.C.A., Salvation Army, American Friends Service Committee, and a host of other Christian organizations. A Hong Kong Discharged Prisoners' Aid Society helps over a thousand discharged prisoners each year.

There is a steady reduction of serious crime in Hong Kong in contrast to other urban areas throughout the world where it is increasing. The government credits this to the law-abiding nature of the Chinese, the increasing integration of the immigrants into the local community, and fuller employment. A third of Hong Kong's prisoners are in open prisons (without yard walls), and ultimately all prisoners with sentences of two years or less will be included in this unique experiment that puts the prisoners in rural areas for forestry and road building work.

Over 60 per cent of Hong Kong's criminals are narcotic addicts. Estimates of the total number of addicts vary from 150,000 to 250,000, or at least one in every twenty of the residents of the colony. Opium addiction has had a long history in the area. The raw opium comes into the colony from the border regions of southern Yunnan and northern Laos, Thailand, and Burma, much of it smuggled by ship from Bangkok. Since the war, with government pressure on addiction, the use of heroin has increased because it is more concentrated and less detectable. Many start on heroin as a relief for pain, or in the mistaken notion that it is an aphrodisiac, or a cure for disease (particularly T.B.). Special police have been increased, an educational pamphlet has been issued, and a new prison for addicts has been opened that includes medical care, supplementary feeding, and outdoor work projects. The government is co-operating with international agencies to control the traffic. Churches also provide opportunities for care, though permanent cure is rare.

An addict, a disillusioned leftist, often cured of his physical craving but as often relapsing in escape from life came to see a missionary one night. He said he was returning the next day, permanently, through the Curtain. To be accepted after a long absence, he felt he would have to carry back useful information, so he had made up a detailed story about the missionary being a paid agent of America and Taiwan sent to buy the hearts of Chinese students. He admitted it was untrue but useful. He was not worried about lying, but only about the possibility that they wouldn't believe him, in which case he would have to return to Hong Kong and would then need a sponsor. He begged the American to act as his sponsor if it became necessary. The missionary agreed, which startled him. He did not go through the Curtain, but came back the next day to talk about it. "Why," he asked, "would you be willing to do it?" He was told that a Christian's reason for helping others has no connection with their deserving it, for "While we were yet sinners, Christ died for us." If men received what they deserved, they'd all be in hell long since. Over a period of years this was the only Christian point that seemed to get under his skin. His friend may never be able to reach the defeated, frightened self inside the many tough layers his experiences have wrapped him in, but it is worth trying. Unless the church can reach such people, it fights a losing battle, for addicts infect society, which is ultimately no stronger than its weakest parts. Evil spreads with a chain reaction, and unless goodness and love spread through society with greater infection and forcefulness, a society decays.

Not enough money is available to solve Hong Kong's problems on a relief basis, providing doles for long lines outside churches and welfare offices. It might please a thoughtless person to see photographs of such generosity, but it would not please God. After spending the money and eating the food, the people would be back in line, soon discovering how to send their children into other lines, how to register under different names, and how to get more by telling taller stories. To avoid this, Hong Kong has a Central Records Office where agencies report those they have helped, identity card numbers are filed, duplication is avoided, and division of responsibility becomes possible. Unfortunately, there are not enough caseworkers available to investigate each case, recommend plans, and do the counseling. What then? Group work is one answer—guiding the refugees to help each other. Increased facilities for training social workers are also needed.

In the post-secondary colleges there are hundreds of needy refugee students. Some of the churches, with the aid of Church World Service, started several college student work projects, shifting from a program of grants to the assigning of students to non-profit organizations and churches for community service. The students work two hours a day, five days a week, and earn their college board and lodging. They touch 23,000 children and underprivileged persons in over ninety projects, including free night schools, literacy classes in labor unions, welfare agencies, boys' and girls' clubs, Sunday school classes, manual work, anything that helps other Chinese. Each dollar is used twice. It helps the student and through him the clientele of the project in which he works. It enables the student to see the church in action as well as the welfare work of the city. It gives him needed training for later professional work. Above all, it strengthens his self-respect; he is earning his own way, working for his own people. The skills of one group of refugees can be used to help another group. The young refugee preparing lessons for underprivileged children does not get into gambling or narcotic addiction.

Need for Social Workers

With the growth of social services, Hong Kong has an increasing need for trained social workers. The University trains some, the government's Social Welfare Department others, but not enough. Chung Chi College and the Baptist college also have training programs in social work. A share of the World Refugee Year funds is being devoted to raising standards of achievement and increasing opportunities in Hong Kong for careers in social work. The churches are concerned and add an invaluable element. Professional standards are needed and refugees' stories must be investigated thoroughly, they are often false, yet the individuals need to be trusted as Christ trusted Matthew or Zaccheus. They need to feel that the strange new society they have entered recognizes that they have a contribution to make. The isolated refugee needs a sense of community, of belonging, as much as he needs food or work. The church, when truly the family of God, can draw such individuals into a movement. So many of those who leave the enforced community on the other side of the Curtain are offered nothing but freedom on this side. Freedom, like air, is something you miss desperately when it is denied you, but something that does not satisfy all your hungers when you have it.

The Political Scene

The political atmosphere of Hong Kong differs from that of Taiwan. It allows a wider variety of less committed and more independent points of view. This irritates the Nationalists and the Communists, both of whom feel that the people of Hong Kong have become stateless, have no love of country, and are materialistic and selfish. There are pressures in Hong Kong that lead in this direction. Hong Kong could not long exist except as a neutral entity useful to both sides. But neutrality can become a habit of mind, a state of indecision and irresponsibility. The churches in Hong Kong do not discuss communism and they avoid the politically complex labor situation. Until recently the Council of Churches accepted only one responsibility: the care of the Christian cemetery—live issues being controversial and divisive.

There is a distinct value in a variety of approaches to the regional and cold war problems that Hong Kong faces. A fluid policy, an open-minded approach is preferable to a flat-footed stance. There is tremendous value in unprejudiced research, and there is value from the Christian point of view in contact with those who call themselves enemies. The world cannot be won for Jesus Christ and his liberating truth by policies of segregation, either of races or nations. Hong Kong is a point of contact between worlds.

The colony is British, yet overwhelmingly Chinese and inescapably international. It is full of emergency needs, yet its problems are long-term ones. Will it have a chance to work

on them? Perhaps. There is no feeling of insecurity at the
moment. Yet Hong Kong knows that time is important, that
an avalanche might break loose and come roaring down. The
early church spread in this mood, conscious that the time was
short, that it was high time to wake out of sleep. It is a good
atmosphere for the church. Paul wrote to Timothy, ". . . be
urgent in season and out of season . . ." Such a feeling is
harmful if it grows out of fear and taut nerves. But Paul was
speaking of the sense of God's readiness to act, and of his
call upon our hands and feet and voices; of his opening of
doors through which, if we do not move, others will. A sense
of crisis is the Christian's natural air, but it is produced not
alone by headlines but by looking frankly at life after reading the *New Testament*. Hong Kong presents a challenge to
the Christian church. The people are conscious that an axe
has been laid to the roots of their old ways of life, and a fire
kindled on their threshing floors, and they long for one who
is to come. Will the church speak in such a place to a deeper
hunger than that for comfort or escape? Will it speak a living, persuasive, nourishing word, which men break like bread
and share with one another, and find good?

✳✳✳ 3 ✳✳✳

THE RELEVANCE OF THE CHURCH

The churches in Hong Kong are growing as everything
else is growing, only faster. Is the growth too rapid? It may
be, since the most rapid growth is not in the older churches
where there are experienced laymen and laywomen to help
assure the adequate training and nurture of the new members. The rate of growth is 13 per cent per year. There are
now over three hundred Protestant congregations in the

colony and an estimated 140,000 members. Roman Catholics probably have an equal number, making up together 9 per cent of population, one of the highest percentages in Asia outside of parts of Indonesia.

Concepts of the Church

The older churches of Hong Kong, though growing more slowly than the new ones, have crowded services and are putting out shoots like strawberry plants. Some have started as many as six branches. But adjustments to the rapid changes in Hong Kong have not been easy. After years of effort the churches have achieved self-support, quiet dignity in worship, and a recognized place in the community, only to be deluged with refugees and strangers who speak differently, pray differently, and bring problems to the congregations. No wonder the first reaction is often defensive. Parents want the churches for the training of their children so that they may grow up together and marry into the right families. The church is made up of human beings with all their frailties, and one of these is to respond slowly to people who are different.

There are three concepts of the church in Hong Kong, as elsewhere. One, referred to above, emphasizes the church's protective function. Its members form a colony of heaven in an alien world. Such a church struggles for its right of religious liberty, for its purity of faith, and to keep its members unspotted from the world. It is the usual view of minority churches in antagonistic environments.

Another concept measures the success of the church in statistical terms, seeking a rapidly enlarging membership through mass evangelism and pressure methods, believing that the acceptance of Jesus Christ by faith is not only the central concern of the church, but the only concern. Many post-war crusades for Christ, using mass communications media and rented halls and professional interpreters, have moved through Asia sowing seed on shallow soil where, unless local churches act quickly, the sun scorches it or the weeds choke it.

A third concept emphasizes the concern of the church for whole communities, for man in the total context of his relationships, remembering that Jesus not only spoke to individuals but wept over Jerusalem, cleansed the temple, and announced to his nation the coming of the kingdom. The first concept of the church leads to withdrawal from the world; the second to occupation of the world without changing it; whereas, the third is extremely difficult in practice. It desires to bring the gospel to bear upon the whole of life, but easily divides its membership at the point where the redemptive Word meets the unredeemed aspects of life.

The psychological and economic needs of the people in Hong Kong produce a hunger and an openness that make preaching a joy, and possibly a temptation. The people want security not only in physical terms but in the sure knowledge of the love of God. Under such conditions, the problem is not how to secure members for a church, but how to solve the complicated and heavy personal problems of each family and individual and still help each to see that the decision to accept comfort and forgiveness also involves decisions to undergo a thorough transformation of life and to welcome Christ into all of the personality and its activities. The new Christians are to accept, obey, take up their crosses, follow, and witness. Inspired intelligence is needed in directing Christian love into the production of strength instead of dependence, into the steps by which Christians in need become Christians who meet needs. There is no security except in mission, and those who turn to God because there is nowhere else to turn must discover that they are thereby turned toward their fellow men.

The Jewish people made their greatest contribution to the world not in periods of prosperity but during and after times of exile, when in sackcloth and ashes they listened to the voice of God and thought deeply about pain and suffering and sin. May not these troubled refugees of Asia, if the church succeeds in stirring their wills and minds as well as their emotions, have much to teach those of us whose Christianity is without cost or serious thought?

Fellowship in the Christian Community

A great deal is being done in Hong Kong for and with children and families. The most difficult problem is the large number who have come into the colony without families. Both the churches and the welfare agencies prefer to deal with people in families. There is a stability about families; one makes a case study and it sticks, one goes to an address and there is someone there. But the solitary, the uprooted, those without relatives or friends, the young men with the hollow eyes, with the temptations, with the hearts burning out from an inflammable mixture of aspiration and unfulfillment, those who shift from here to there and are therefore called "shiftless," who cares for them? Hong Kong has an unusual number of these, but it is chiefly unusual in another respect. There is always a way out, available and close—a man can go back through the Curtain, make public confession of error, and be reinstated in the fixed security he has left.

Responsible choice is one of the taxing burdens of freedom. Most North Americans however, are not faced daily with a choice between worlds. For an individual without a family who has recently moved to Hong Kong from a collectivized social life where he was controlled and watched, where decision meant acceptance, thinking meant response, where all crossroads had guideposts, and choice meant merely a firmer gripping of the cable beneath the cable car, freedom can be an invitation to disaster.

How do we explain the glorious liberty of the children of God to those who are easily weakened by the spurious liberty of the children of men? The answer, of course, is in the fellowship of the Christian community, where sinful men are being saved together, where humble men realize that they depend upon God, upon each other, and upon a constant sharing with non-Christians of the faith that upholds them. The answer for men who cannot stand alone is found in the close company of men who stand together for the things of God. A healthy church is a demonstration of a voluntary disciplined community of mutual burden bearing and common witness, with Christ at the center, in which free men learn to make decisions and subordinate their selfishness within the pattern of his purpose to redeem the whole of life.

Non-Christian Confrontation

What is the religious environment in which the churches work? Buddhism is the strongest of the local faiths. There are old Buddhist temples, prominent Buddhist families, and able laymen. Buddhist priests are called into homes to officiate at weddings and funerals, and the Buddhist Association does charitable work and has a few schools and publications. There are a number of monasteries as well as homes for Buddhist single women. Taoism and Islam are not very active, and Confucianism, though maintaining an intellectual hold, is no longer a religion. These several influences are the source of a continuing struggle between the generations, for the parents demand the old rites at their funerals, publicly participated in by their children as evidence of filial devotion, whereas the children are often indifferent.

A Christian Study Center, sponsored by the World Council of Churches, aids the churches in understanding and in making relevant contact with the non-Christian religions. It is of great potential importance if the churches are to help liberate Chinese society without loss of abiding values. At present the center is handicapped by lack of resources in funds and personnel.

None of the other religious groups are growing as rapidly as the Christian churches, nor is any other faith as effective in influencing children and youth. Buddhism denies the reality of the suffering and sin the people see around them, and offers escape from social responsibility into holiness and peace by way of the fourfold path of virtue. But there are youth who are not interested in thinking away the suffering and sin and finding peace only for themselves. They want peace for their people and righteousness for all through a cure of the disease rather than the symptoms; through a genuine removal of the causes of the sin and suffering. Here there are only two options: Marxism and Christianity. These two approaches differ in both diagnosis and treatment. The one sees the cause in a rotten society and the cure as lying within the will of men directed by the Communist party; the other sees the cause in the corrupted will of man that has infected society, and the cure in God's costly act of forgiveness and in his regenerating power that restores man to cooperation with him, both in redeeming life and using to the full its resources.

There is a Hong Kong Christian Council representing Chinese and English churches and missions, and a Chinese Christian Churches Union for the Chinese clergy. The Christian Council sponsors the Hong Kong Christian Welfare and Relief Council, whose twenty-four Protestant churches and interdenominational agencies co-ordinate many of the church's welfare projects. It reports local needs through the World Council of Churches.

Students

College and university students are subject to the ideological pressures that affect the rim of Asia and the temptations that abound in a port city like Hong Kong. An active ministry to students and youth is essential. They will become a lost generation if they fail to find understanding and purpose that gives shape to the freedom Hong Kong offers. Extremism of the right or the left, narcotic addiction, and many other antisocial possibilities are present. It would be tragic to let youth's assets be wasted because society makes no call upon their skills or sense of vocation. Fortunately the churches of Hong Kong have strong youth programs and the Student Christian Movement is active.

A Student Christian Center, directed by an ecumenical committee, was opened in Hong Kong in 1957 and attracts thousands of college students each month. Its cornerstone reads, "None Other Foundation than Jesus Christ." The Center was founded in faith, not only faith in God, but faith in youth. It was erected in hope that within its walls youth might find a true center for their lives and that their character might be rounded out and furnished with those elements of strength, integrity, courtesy, and consideration that make a man. It is a place that students living on hillsides and in dark crowded sleeping quarters can call their own; where they meet for discussion, recreation, prayer, music, jobs, and friendship.

The Center is nonpolitical; no one seeks to buy the hearts of the students, to secure control of their thoughts, to manipulate or use them for ulterior ends. They are treated with respect as free men and are welcome whether or not they come with pressed clothing and recent haircuts. The Student Christian Movement, World University Service, the Committee on College Work Projects, and an Emergency Service Fund Committee use the Center as their headquarters. In the dedication of the Center, prayer was offered that students who entered it might keep faith with those who loved and trusted them and whose hopes followed them; that those who were alone and confused might have the reassuring knowledge of God as Father. That prayer has been answered many times, and it will continue to be answered many times more as the Center extends its service.

Yet, still, in Hong Kong there are students like the one who wrote in 1954 to a newspaper stating that after reaching Hong Kong he lived in a refugee camp and sold "his physical labor at a cut price." After three years of struggle he contracted tuberculosis, but had no money to enter a hospital. So he wrote a cry for help, closing with these words, "the upheavals of this period may cause the death of countless numbers of unfortunate people, for no good reason. I am not a popular hero or a pillar of my nation and if I die from illness in a foreign land the world will not miss me. From this point of view, the best thing to do is to accept the will of heaven or fate. But I come back again to the fact that I am yet a man, and I hope that through the vast misfortunes of human life I can continue the thread of this my own life."

Human Need and the Church

Wherever in the world there are unmet human needs, the church is concerned. The needs may be physical, emotional, spiritual—it doesn't matter. The church, in the name of the Son of Man, is concerned with the whole man, not a part only. The church is a redemptive movement in which every member in every pew can participate actively. In a place like Hong Kong, with thousands of temporarily underprivileged people, the church must heal and teach and counsel and rehabilitate.

How is the evangelistic work of the church to be related to its practical welfare activities? This is still an unsolved problem for churches throughout the world. It demands our attention. Jesus faced the problem in his temptations and throughout his ministry. The people would have responded in larger numbers if he had provided more bread and healing. He did care about their hunger and their health, but he often urged those he healed to tell no one. He did not want people to follow him for the benefits, but because they understood him, had faith in him, and were willing to bear their own crosses and work with him. The church should not do social work for the sake of winning converts. It should not separate the two forms of witness, as though it proclaimed on Sunday a personal gospel but demonstrated on weekdays a social gospel. The cup of cold water is given in the name of Jesus Christ. It points beyond the giver to the love that is God's nature, and points beyond the receiver to the others with whom God's gifts are to be shared.

Giving by sinful men easily creates resentment. The offering must be set in humility and tempered with deep appreciation of the recipient's contribution to life. The problem is to find relief workers who can give, in addition to material

things, the look in the eye that Peter and John gave the crip-
ple, the word of confidence and faith that puts the recipient
on his feet.

The Western Christian and Hong Kong

Two daily experiences weigh heavily on the spirit of a
Western Christian in Hong Kong. One is contact with need
greater than all that combined Christian effort can meet.
The other is the constant impingement of words and expressions of face that hide rather than reveal. No one likes to be
confused or to suspect others. A Christian must try to trust
the worst of sinners, yet not be taken in and exploited. The
effort to trust and to give the nourishing gift of confidence,
and at the same time to be thinking, analyzing, distinguish-
ing the true from the false, is exacting and tiring. A Christian
may long for a simple environment where words are not
counterfeit, where motives can be assessed, and where one
meets only such simple sins as murder, alcoholism, and theft.
Hong Kong is filled with sturdy, wonderful people. It is also
filled with the hunted, the haunted, and the broken. War,
revolution, and political struggle produce both types. The
church must be open to both. But membership and partak-
ing of the sacraments involve decision and a change of life.
Can the church maintain its spiritual vitality and the purity
of its witness if it fills its pews with those who have been
broken morally? It can, if the whole congregation under-
stands its mission.

The climate in Hong Kong is such that if good seeds are
not sown, weeds will spring up rapidly. The time is short. All
over Asia there is an intense effort to foreshorten the process
of change, to force the pace, to exceed goals, and accomplish
plans ahead of time. It has been said, "Blessed are the pace-

makers, for theirs is the ultimate society." China wants to outrun and leave behind the decadent and planless West. Communists insist that the Christian church has had two thousand years to meddle with the world and try to change it, but has only halfheartedly bothered with the matter and now wants it left as it is. The church must, therefore, give way to men who mean business.

It is not that the West is not busy. It is rushing about making money, building houses and churches, nervously watching the world on television, advertising its consumer goods to its own people and its weapons to those who already fear it —but where is it going? If the West shares any belief with others, it is that life, liberty, and the pursuit of happiness are inalienable rights. But if the interpretation of this creed is that life's meaning lies in the liberty to pursue one's own happiness, it is scarcely an exhaustive statement of a faith that could be the foundation of a reconciled world. It fails to hear the whole creation groaning and travailing together until the sons of God appear.

Western Christians are being goaded by history and events to think about the meaning of life and what men ultimately seek. In economies of scarcity and in areas of dissatisfaction, we do not fare well when we offer freedom with no interpretation of the past, no convincing analysis of the present, and no clear steps for the future. We are in competition with a messianic intellectual and social revolution that moves with the momentum of intolerant confidence. America has been pushed awkwardly into the center of a battlefield clutching only a butter knife instead of a sword of the spirit. This battle is in the mind and heart and social purposes of man, not in the atomic laboratories. What doth it profit a nation to destroy the whole world and lose its own soul?

All of these strictures on Western action must, of course, be balanced by the realization that world communism is riddled with internal contradictions and has been blinded by its sense of urgency into adopting methods that are self-defeating. But, who wants to sit and watch while acids of hatred and internal suspicion work their inevitable corrosion?

Hong Kong is important as a microcosm in which two worlds meet; as a small stage on which protagonists of both sides walk into each other; as a place where the consciousness that each day may be the last day underlines the relevance of eternal truth to the immediate present; as a place where neglected truth may surprise and disturb, reopening closed issues, ambushing guarded hearts, and humbling stubborn minds.

YOU AND THE RIM OF EAST ASIA

Have you ever tried to see how many marbles you could put, one by one, in a flat pan balanced on your head? The balance on the rim of East Asia is just as precarious as that. Each year more people, more problems, more pressures are added, and no one knows when one further addition will cause the whole thing to tip completely to left or right. But there are other ways of using heads than playing parlor games with them. John Dewey called the human brain a tool for the solving of problems. In a world engaged in an ideological war, involving conflicting ways of life, to have a kind heart and a blank mind is to invite disaster.

North Americans can escape from the problems of the inner city into the suburbs. But there are no suburbs left in the world situation. Where can you go to escape the problems of Laos, Cuba, Algeria, the Congo, Taiwan, and the other areas that will become "hot" between this writing and your reading?

The eighteenth century was called the Age of Reason. The present one is not the Space Age, as it is often called, but truly the Age of Dilemmas. Today, the mind is taxed as heavily as the pocketbook. We must mix thinking with our prayer. God requires an accounting of the stewardship of our intelligence. We in the West are deeply involved in East Asia as helping hands and as sources of irritation. We are our own

worst enemies. Why? Look at the common, recurring, unsolved problems:

(1) *Foreign Aid.* Foreign aid is a necessity if we are
Christian, and a necessity if we are not; without it, the world
situation will become seriously worse. The aid is essential,
appreciated, and resented. No one likes to feel dependent, or
to feel like a puppet. In South Korea, Okinawa, and Taiwan
we have unintentionally created a semicolonial situation in
which the military, political, and economic security of these
countries rests upon decisions made thousands of miles away
in Washington, Ottawa, New York, and elsewhere. The
American colonies fought a revolutionary war because they
did not like taxation without representation. In East Asia the
same effect is produced by the opposite of taxation—aid—
suggesting that the irritation arises from a common element,
the helplessness and unpredictability arising from dependence upon foreign decisions. The aid program also offers a
constant temptation to skip over slower, sounder ways of
development, thus providing opportunities for corruption.

Should foreign aid be cut? No. It should be used with intelligent interest in Asian desires and needs, and with more
respect for Asian cultural patterns. Much of the money is
now well used, and there are able administrators who have
worked miracles. But tremendous problems are involved
when successful executives from an economy of plenty seek
to administer aid in an economy of scarcity. Dependent
upon interpreters, advisers, officials, it is not easy for them to
get the nuances of the language, to live and think as the local
people do, to sense directly the reactions of the Asians. Every
effort should be made to shift from the easier programs of
relief to the more difficult projects that enable people to solve
their own problems.

(2) *Military Aid.* Asians want security and therefore many of them appreciate our military aid. Yet it builds up an establishment out of proportion to the local tax income and industrial potential. Military bases take food-producing land from the people, creating resentment regardless of the compensation offered. Asian peace sentiment, also, is strong and many are disturbed by the militarization the West finances. Asians know that such aid is not entirely disinterested, and that it endangers even while it protects, since it causes apprehension in other countries. Military aid is a stop-gap and offers no permanent solution for the people's problems.

(3) *The Moral Situation.* The demonstrations of Western self-interest are now on a larger scale in Asia than are Christian demonstrations. Too few servicemen, tourists, businessmen, and diplomats are sensitive to local moral standards. A society may be lax from a Western point of view, yet view with moral condemnation habits the West considers relatively harmless. We must reread Paul's discussion of eating food that had been offered to idols and remember his concern not to cause others to stumble. This counsel is important for all entering the Peace Corps or other overseas services and for every citizen here or abroad. The world mission of the church now depends upon the faith and example of laymen who follow Christ in their secular occupations. Along the rim of East Asia the faith was often planted by sailors, traders, diplomats, and scholars.

(4) *Relief Work and Christian Evangelism.* The relief of *immediate* human needs and the satisfaction of man's *eternal* hunger for acceptance with God are so often related in a false way that this remains a primary religious problem wherever the church ministers to underprivileged people.

(5) *Relief and Rehabilitation.* Since the Japanese moved

into Manchuria in 1931, there has been war along the rim of
East Asia, sometimes hot, sometimes cold, but always producing tension and insecurity and movement of people. The
effect on the nerves, bodies, and morals has been disastrous.
Agencies of compassion are blind if all they provide now is
food, clothing, and housing. The people need to be understood, to be forgiven, and to forgive. They need to tell their
stories to sympathetic ears, to pull up from the dark wells of
memory their experiences and sufferings and hatreds so they
may look at them and forget them. They need to lose their
sense of alienation and exile in a new found experience of
community where they are wanted, employed, and loved.
They need to stop feeling driven and have time to think, re-
evaluate life, and enjoy neighbors with common interests,
instead of forever appraising and competing with strangers.
They need the security of realization that the universe is
firmly held in the hands of God who, through his crucified
and risen Son, has shown men the cruelty and futility of
their attempts to take the kingdom by climbing over the wall
on the bodies of those they purged for being in the way, yet
has opened wide to them the peaceable kingdom of their true
desire. They need the message and membership an awakened
and faithful church can give them. If the church does not
give these, because too many of its members are using its
ministry as aspirin for their own ills and have no intention of
entering the mighty movement of God's Spirit to reconcile
and redeem this broken world, then how great is its responsibility!

(6) *Unity*. Divisive tendencies are harming both church
and nation in Korea and Taiwan. The Biblical and theological reasons why it is sinful to divide the body of Christ need
to be stressed more than the practical reasons. The false

claim that the World Council of Churches and the movement toward reunion are seeking a superchurch with totalitarian control over all the branches and uniformity in thought and worship must be countered with sounder education and literature in Korean and Chinese.

(7) *Challenge, Training, and Nurture.* With evangelism relatively easy on the rim of East Asia, the churches must immediately strengthen their programs to train and call into effective witness and service the many who are accepting Jesus Christ. The effort to produce relevant Christian education materials on the spot, in the vernacular rather than translated, should be fully supported. Theological seminaries need thoughtful planning and enlarging, and the Bible schools should be related to them wherever possible so that they do not work at cross-purposes.

(8) *Population.* Along the rim of East Asia the population is growing too rapidly for the food producing capacity of the land. Japan has faced the problem and is working toward a stable, stationary population in a few years, but she is permitting early abortion, which is dangerous. Medical and educational missionaries particularly should be prepared to explore with Asians all healthy avenues of solution if we want the people of the world to avoid a blind alley.

(9) *Democracy.* The democratic way of life needs to be given a clearer, more universal content. There are elements in it that grow out of a Christian view of God and man, and other elements and political structures that grow out of the trial and error of local experience and may not be practicable in a different culture, or under different historical conditions. These need to be disentangled, lest North American Christians find themselves implanting a Western way of life in Asia where only an Eastern version of democracy could put

down roots, becoming in fact cultural imperialists. Men are needed who can think within the given terms of another situation about the essentials of a good life, who are not bound by the concepts of their own culture nor vague and unable to give form to new expressions of faith in freedom. There are permanent and biblically grounded values in freedom of choice, the acceptance of personal responsibility, the concern for a community of love rather than of mere coercion, the protection of minorities, the proper balancing of rights and duties, and the practice of forgiveness. Church members in Asia, as elsewhere, need courteous help in discerning the implications of the Christian view of life, and should not be carelessly pushed into acceptance of political forms that fit other situations, nor be offered talk about freedom that has no content.

(10) *Reciprocity*. The West will not be well liked in Asia until it becomes less conscious of what it has to give and more conscious of what it is receiving and learning in its common struggle with Asians against the enemies of man: poverty, hunger, disease, and sin. I remember a student with tuberculosis whom I helped slightly. When well enough to travel, he went home. Weeks later, a letter came stating that Mr. Chang's sick mother had insisted he help support the two parents. He had gone to Shanghai where he finally committed suicide. Before doing so he had asked an acquaintance to write and ask me if I wanted his textbooks and clothing. I replied that I would like to have them and was terribly sorry to hear of Mr. Chang's death. A week later a letter arrived from Mr. Chang stating that his suicide was a test case. He couldn't find work and was friendless. He remembered me but, thinking I had forgotten him, staged the suicide. My wanting his possessions proved that I remembered him, so

the suicide was off, he was indeed not friendless and he would continue to live. It is a strange story, perhaps, but it shows that valuing a human being in a personal way—even including his possessions—can make the difference for him between life and death. The greatest need of refugees is to feel that they are not discarded, but have a contribution to make that the world would be poorer without. The church can open to them the family life of an interdependent Christian community with work for everyone. To do this the church must be in movement in all areas of life, involved in mission as an ever witnessing, worshiping, working fellowship of those who live not unto themselves but unto Him.

The dilemmas and unsolved problems are many, but are not grounds for discouragement. It may be some comfort to remember that there are contradictions in every human effort. The Communist movement that seems to move so surely is riddled with inner contradictions. The party offers with one hand what it takes away with the other. The land hunger of peasants is used to liquidate landlords, the land is divided, then nationalized and the peasants collectivized so that no one owns land but the state. All citizens are drawn into democratic discussion of national issues and told to express themselves freely, only to be caught out on the limb of their own expression when reports are made later and the purges begin. The hunger for community is aroused, but an extreme form of individualism is produced by creating mutual suspicion through required reporting of all deviation (even of father, husband, or colleague) and labeling it treason. Each individual learns to censor himself and submerge all thoughts that do not agree with the radio and the newspaper. Communication becomes formal and each person lives in a private world, isolated even from part of himself.

But Christians are warned not to seek consolation in analyzing the inner contradictions of others. "Love rejoiceth not in [others'] iniquity." When we find ourselves in dilemmas caused in part by our own self-deceiving or self-defeating ways, the way out is through our own repentance and reconversion, through clearer thinking, selfless praying, and closer following of Him who was tempted as we are, yet without sin.

The church can do certain things in East Asia that no government can. Harassed people who have been treated as means to political ends need the healing discovery that Christ considers each of them worth the death on the cross. They need to discover that aid given in his name is not publicized to further anyone's national or ecclesiastical aims, but is given for their own sake and his, that they may live significantly. There are broken lives all along the rim of East Asia that must be made whole again, severed ideas that can only be reassembled and joined around a new perspective, blunted vocational skills that need sharpening, wounds that only the love of God in Christ and men can heal. The United Nations and government agencies can work out the larger details of a solution, but they cannot do the listening, the binding up of broken hearts, the patient counseling, the trying of one method after another, the encouraging with hope and faith, the assuring of forgiveness and cleansing. Only the personal attention of those who have learned to practice the presence of God can do this. Christians are needed, with the very best that the church can contribute in the way of intelligence, devotion, skill, and prayer.

The church's need for missionaries and fraternal workers continues. The New Testament call has not been withdrawn. New needs are being created by new situations. The missionary today finds that his welcome is more dependent than formerly upon world news and the public mood. He will be appreciated one year and attacked another as representing Western interests and old injustices. He must have a love that "is not easily provoked," that "thinks no evil," that "bears all things, believes all things, hopes all things, endures all things." In an age of interchurch relations, the relations depend ultimately, not on letters, visits, and the exchange of specialists, but on those who offer their lives, learn the languages, get the grassroots of the adopted land between their toes, and become living dictionaries of the meaning of the ecumenical relationship.

In what ways can we help? By praying, supporting, reading, and participating sensitively in the world mission, of which our local church's witness and our own is a part. By urging our children's schools to teach world history, world geography, and current events, as though the world deserved our attention and the intelligent preparation of youth for participation in its affairs. By setting our Sunday schools and church youth and men's and women's groups more clearly in the context of mission, so that they pass beyond the imparting of knowledge to the provision of historical and biblical perspectives and a logic for action that we can all take within the ecumenical mission of the church. By serious work to overcome race prejudice and all inequalities that contradict our faith, harm people, and slow up the world mission. By preparing and introducing Christian participants in the Peace Corps, Crossroads Africa, and similar ventures to the churches overseas so that there may be a strengthening of ties and they may return with a new vision of the world task of the church. By welcoming the foreign students and foreign residents in our communities into our homes and churches that we may learn from each other and make more personal our interest in other peoples. You can think of other ways to help—and should.

But why bother? Well—consider the alternatives to an active, reconciling mission. If the church loses confidence in Christ's methods of love and faith, is no longer certain that God is the Lord of history, and is convinced that the kingdom is not going to come on earth, then it will give up the field in a defensive retreat, leaving Asia and Africa to those who believe in other weapons. That would mean either a new isolationism and splitting of the world into armed fortresses with no communication (for communication would mean subversion), or mutual atomic destruction with bleak prospects for a few survivors. Either Jesus Christ has cosmic support and is the Way, the Truth and the Life—or he does not, and is not, and we do not believe in him. It is as simple as that. The issues are drawn, the choices are before us. We are either of those who shrink back, or of those who have faith. The Christian mission must be strengthened and carried forward, or given up, if we are to be consistent. We can give our lives in trying to save the peoples of the world in the name of Jesus Christ, or we can try to save our own lives and lose them ingloriously. Do we follow the One who set His face steadfastly toward Jerusalem, knowing that a cross was ahead?

READING LIST

Leaders of study groups may order the Friendship Press books listed below from denominational literature headquarters. From these same sources, they may also order the *Adult Guide on the Rim of East Asia*, by Isobel McFadden, priced at 75 cents, which contains program plans for using *On Asia's Rim* and other Friendship Press materials.

Books of other publishers are listed as additional resources. They are available in bookstores and libraries.

FRIENDSHIP PRESS BOOKS

Billings, Peggy. *The Waiting People*. Four short stories point up the representative problems facing young people on Asia's rim. 1962. Cloth $2.95, paper $1.75.

Dahlberg, Edwin T. *This Is the Rim of East Asia*. An illustrated primer for young people and adults. 1962. Paper only, 85 cents.

Jones, Francis Price. *The Church in Communist China: A Protestant Appraisal*. A thought provoking analysis of Christian behavior in a Communist society. 1962. Cloth $3.50, paper $1.95.

Moffett, Samuel Hugh. *The Christians of Korea*. A popular review of a fervent, growing but divided church. Photographically illustrated. 1962. Cloth $2.95, paper $1.95.

Introducing Animism by Eugene Nida and *Introducing Buddhism* by Kenneth Scott Latourette. Useful background reading on the four countries on Asia's rim—Korea, Okinawa, Taiwan, and Hong Kong. 1959, 1956. Paper only, 90 cents.

BOOKS OF OTHER PUBLISHERS

General

American Academy of Political and Social Science. *America and a New Asia*. (*Annals*, Vol. 294, July, 1954). Philadelphia, The American Academy . . . , 1954.

Cressey, George Babcock. *Asia's Lands and Peoples*. N.Y.: McGraw-Hill Book Co., Inc., rev. ed., 1951.

Hughes, Ernest Richard and Hughes, K. *Religion in China*. N.Y.: Rinehart and Co., Inc., 1950.

Reischauer, Edwin O. and Fairbank, John K. *East Asia: The Great Tradition* (History of East Asian Civilization, Vol. 1). Boston: Houghton Mifflin Co., 1960.

Korea

Chung, Kyung Cho. *Korea Tomorrow, Land of the Morning Calm*. N.Y.: The Macmillan Co., 1956.

Keith, Elizabeth. *Old Korea, the Land of Morning Calm*. N.Y.: Philosophical Library, Inc., 1947.

Kim, Agnes Davis. *I Married a Korean*. N.Y.: John Day Co., Inc., 1953.

Kim, So-Un. *The Story Bag: A Collection of Korean Folk Tales*. Rutland, Vt.: Charles E. Tuttle Co., 1955.

Korea: Its Land, People and Culture of All Ages. (Published originally by Hakwon-Sa, Ltd., Seoul, Korea.) So. Pasadena, Calif.: Hutchins Oriental Books, 1960.

McCune, George M. and Grey, Arthur L. Jr. *Korea Today*. Cambridge, Mass.: Harvard University Press, 1950.

McCune, Shannon. *Korea's Heritage: A Regional and Social Geography*. Rutland, Vt.: Charles E. Tuttle Co., 1956.

Osgood, Cornelius B. *Koreans and Their Culture*. New York: The Ronald Press Co., 1951.

Weems, Clarence Norwood. *Korea: Dilemma of an Underdeveloped Country* (Headline Series, no. 144, Nov./Dec. 1960). N.Y.: Foreign Policy Assoc., 1960.

Okinawa

Glacken, Clarence J. *The Great Loochoo: A Study of Okinawa Village Life*. Berkeley, Calif.: University of California Press, 1955.

Higa, Gasei (comp.). *Tours of Okinawa: A Souvenir Guide*. Rutland, Vt.: Charles E. Tuttle Co., 1959.

Kerr, George H. *Okinawa: The History of an Island People*. Rutland, Vt.: Charles E. Tuttle Co., 1958.

Zabilka, Gladys. *Customs and Culture of Okinawa*. Rutland, Vt.: Charles E. Tuttle Co., rev. ed., 1959.

Taiwan

Ballentine, Joseph William. *Formosa, A Problem for United States Foreign Policy*. Washington, D.C.: The Brookings Institute, 1952.

Barclay, George W. *Colonial Development and Population in Taiwan*. Princeton, N.J.: Princeton University Press, 1954.

Riggs, Fred Warren. *Formosa Under Chinese Nationalist Rule*. New York: The Macmillan Co., 1952.

Hong Kong

Davis, S. G. *Hong Kong in Its Geographical Setting*. N.Y.: British Book Center, 1950.

Endacott, George B. *A History of Hong Kong*. N.Y.: Oxford University Press, 1958.

Rand, Christopher. *Hong Kong, the Island Between*. N.Y.: Alfred A. Knopf, Inc., 1952.

ABOUT THE FORMAT

The text of this book is set in 11 point Electra
leaded 2 points. It is an original type face, not based
upon any traditional model, designed by the eminent
American artist and illustrator W. A. Dwiggins.
Manufactured by Book Craftsmen Associates, Inc., New York
Jackets and paper covers by Affiliated Lithographers, Inc.,
New York
Text paper: S. D. Warren's #66 Antique
Typographic design by Warren Johnson
Binding by Louise E. Jefferson

$2.95

ON ASIA'S RIM

by Andrew T. Roy

Jacket design by Andrew Ho

Andrew T. Roy's book opens a window upon thirty-eight million people crowded together on Asia's rim. They are people who deserve the immediate attention of the West for two reasons: first, in their own right; and second, because what happens to them affects world destiny.

In vivid prose Dr. Roy paints the historical, economic, political, and religious picture in Korea, Okinawa, Taiwan, and Hong Kong. **On Asia's Rim** sets the church squarely in the midst of the problems of fifteen million refugees; of the pros and cons of foreign aid; of freedom in a world of power politics; of reconstruction from the havoc of war and revolution. Decisions made in Peking and Moscow, in Washington and Ottawa and London, and in the United Nations intimately affect the people of East Asia; the church cannot abstract itself from the consequences of such decisions.

The Christians on Asia's rim are relatively few. They cannot be expected to pull Western chestnuts out of the Asian fire or work sudden miracles of statesmanship, but they do make up a minority that is active and creative. They are generally better educated than their neighbors and better able to see beyond their own immediate needs. Like the small and struggling Christian groups of Augustine's day, they constitute